ITALIANS

OF

NEWARK

ITALIANS

OF

NEWARK

· A HISTORY ·

ANDREA LYN CAMMARATO-VAN BENSCHOTEN

Foreword by Patrick A. O'Boyle, Esq., co-host of the Italian American Podcast

THE
History
PRESS

Published by The History Press
Charleston, SC
www.historypress.com

Front cover, clockwise from top left: Shoeshine on Garside Street in the First Ward in 1930. *Courtesy of Gerard Zanfini and Michael D. Immerso First Ward Italian collection; Charles F. Cummings New Jersey Information Center, Newark Public Library*; Procession of the Feast of St. Anthony in 1906. *Courtesy of Gerard Zanfini and Michael D. Immerso First Ward Italian collection; Charles F. Cummings New Jersey Information Center, Newark Public Library*; Children sitting with their mother at the rear of a tenement in the First Ward of Newark. *Courtesy of Gerard Zanfini and Michael D. Immerso First Ward Italian collection; Charles F. Cummings New Jersey Information Center, Newark Public Library*; Boys playing on Mount Prospect Avenue, circa 1945. *Courtesy of Annette Zarra CiFalino of Nutley; Gerard Zanfini and Michael D. Immerso First Ward Italian collection; Charles F. Cummings New Jersey Information Center, Newark Public Library*; Lucia Di Biase Fucetola, who arrived in the United States in 1902. *Courtesy of Andrea Lyn Cammarato-Van Benschoten.*

Back cover, top: Members of Societa' Fraterno Amore (Caposelese Society) pose on Eighth Avenue at the intersection of Nesbit Street in 1924. *Courtesy of Gerard Zanfini and Michael D. Immerso First Ward Italian collection; Charles F. Cummings New Jersey Information Center, Newark Public Library*; *inset*: Ettore Victor "Sonny" Fieramosca in 1955. Born in Newark in 1923, Uncle Sonny grew up on Cutler Street and was a maintenance worker at Stephen Crane Village for thirty-two years. *Courtesy of Andrea Lyn Cammarato-Van Benschoten.*

First published 2024

Manufactured in the United States

ISBN 9781467155960

Library of Congress Control Number: 2024938194

I dedicate this book to my family members who have gone to eternal rest before me. They are in my prayers, and not a day goes by that I don't think about them. When my husband and I first looked at what is now our home, I looked at a wall in the hallway and thought to myself I could finally do a family photo wall. Photos of family members my husband and I hold most dear now hang on the wall and help us recall happy times. We get to see them every day and smile.

CONTENTS

Contents

CONTENTS

FOREWORD

Some things in life are impossible to imagine. A child cannot really conceive what it is like to get old. Some things in life are impossible to imagine. Who driving the roads in the late 1980s could have conceived that the map in their glove compartment would be replaced by GPS? Some things in life are impossible to imagine. In the final years of the 1940s, who could have imagined that Newark's Italian American community, the fifth largest in the United States, in half a century would be decimated to but a handful? At the time, that thought was as ridiculous as it was unimaginable. Yet that sad scenario came to be.

But the extinction of Italian Newark may be a misperception. Cemeteries are filled with abandoned graves, overrun with weeds and devoid of flowers; they are filled with decrepit gravestones, crumbling and covered illegible inscriptions. The names of those buried there are as forgotten as their life stories. The good times and the bad, regardless, are lost to history. The message they send to the passerby is "Does or why would anyone care?"

But the stories of those cemeteries are misread. Those buried in those graves are very much alive. Their descendants may range into the thousands; the further descended the generation, the more people who inhabit the earth who have their eyes, or their nose, or their gift to play the violin, or their receding hairline at a young age. Their last names, a letter added here, a letter taken there, cover the drivers' licenses of their progeny when they themselves left this earth in the age of the horse and carriage. The reality of the dead does not define the vitality of their children.

With Italian Newark, the story is very much the same. Italian Newark has grown, spread and evolved. Italian Newark no longer lives on Sheffield Street or Garside Street. It lives in the Caldwells, in the towns of the Jersey Shore, in newly developed communities in Florida. It is there, very much alive; it is just hard to find in the city of Newark itself.

The descendants of the first Italian immigrants of Newark, if gathered in one place, would populate a place much bigger than the city of Newark itself. They have taken their identity—their traditions and their culture—and brought it far and wide across the United States and even in instances across the world. They remember; they do not forget. They have done what their ancestors did—left a home they loved for a better life for their children. In this way, there is no way that they could not more be like their Italian ancestors.

It's important to take children to see the graves of their ancestors; it teaches them where they came from, who they came from and what they are. To live today, they need to know what has made them what they are, the same for the Italians of Newark. They have continued their Newark Italian traditions now in different places. They may have never been to Newark and be removed many generations from living there, yet Italian Newark lives on in them.

Commendatore Avvocato Professore Patrick A. DiPaula O'Boyle, Esq.
Co-Host of the *Italian American Podcast*

GRAZIE

As this project has finally come to fruition, there are a number of people I need to thank.

First, I need to thank Gabriele and Lucia Fucetola, Ettore Victor and Rosaria Fieramosca, Santo and Concetta Cammarato and Michele and Angelia Palmieri, my great-grandparents, who decided to risk everything and come to the United States to begin anew. Without them, I would not be here to tell this story. I've been researching my family for a long time. The proliferation of online databases has made research less challenging in many cases, and for that I am grateful. I was asked a philosophical question a while back that people sometimes ask at parties: "If you could share a meal with anyone, who would it be and why?" Most people involved in the conversation mentioned famous singers, athletes and actors. I said, "I would like to meet one of my great-grandparents so I can ask what made them decide to leave behind all they knew to come to America." As I sometimes do, I brought a lighthearted conversation to a screeching halt.

I am eternally grateful to those who were so willing to share the immigration stories of their families. No matter the family history, three themes rang true: faith, family and food. These stories came from different people whose families settled in Newark when they first arrived in the United States. They did not know each other, but the strength of those themes showed me what our heritage really is. As this project came together, I could feel their pride and appreciation for those ancestors who decided to build a new life in

America, and they are doing all they can to stay true to their heritage and honor it every day.

I need to thank my Aunt Roslyn for her support. Roslyn Fieramosca-Bolcato, my mother's sister, the person I now refer to as "my adultier adult," is the person I still turn to for guidance and advice. Her sharp mind, ability to recall even the smallest of details and never-ending family stories have filled my heart and mind. For that I will always be grateful.

The staff at the Charles F. Cummings New Jersey Information Center at the Newark Public Library has been an amazing source of information. I am sure my constant emails, calls and visits became challenging over time. I appreciate the additional time they spent helping me identifying resources, acquiring scans and providing suggestions. If people wonder if libraries are still a worthwhile community investment, believe me, they are.

The book that sparked my interest a long time ago was Michael Immerso's *Newark's Little Italy: The Vanished First Ward*. When Michael's book first came out, I took my grandmother to hear him speak. I made sure we arrived early so she could sit up front and hear everything. When the Q&A commenced at the end of his lecture, there were a few questions he couldn't quite answer. My grandmother began to feed him information. At one point he joked, "I'm being coached here." After the event was over, she had a line of people eager to talk to her about "the old neighborhood." Michael, your book has a special place in my library and helped create a unique memory for me while making my grandmother feel incredibly special. I also appreciate you sharing your family story with me so I can somewhat return the favor for all you have done for our community.

Three additional individuals who were critical in finding historical records, sharing personal knowledge and providing key encouragement are the curator of the Museum of the Old First Ward, Bob Cascella; the director of the Italian Apostolate, Cavaliere (Cav.) Professore (Prof.) Eric Lavin; and Very Reverend Cavaliere (Cav.) Thomas D. Nicastro, VF, pastor of St. Mary's Church of Nutley and chaplain for the Italian Apostolate. Bob, Eric and Father Nicastro provided key support, especially as the deadline began to loom large. I truly appreciate your continued assistance and enthusiasm for this project.

I want to sincerely thank the co-hosts of *The Italian American Podcast* for their inspiration and continued education to our community. As the older generation of my family passed one by one, I felt like my heritage was slowly starting to slip away. It left me feeling incredibly despondent. As I began a more concentrated focus on my genealogy research in an effort to reconnect to the family I lost, I looked for resources to further that connection to my heritage. *The Italian American Podcast* was a big part of that connection. It led me to become a member of various Italian American groups, join southern Italy genealogy groups and subscribe to the *Italian Tribune*. It helped me find a new community of others like me, individuals who see value in preserving our heritage amid dwindling families and reduced free time. What I've learned is there are many more of us out there than I realized. Thank you for that.

A special standout as a co-host of *The Italian American Podcast* for me is Comm. Avv. Prof. Patrick A. DiPaula O'Boyle, Esq. A fellow New Jersey native and Gen-Xer, his seemingly endless knowledge on a variety of topics is incredibly impressive. Given our similar upbringing in a multigenerational household, his obvious love for his grandmother and, as I learned, our growing up only a few towns away from each other, hearing him talk about his upbringing was like hearing from an old friend. Pat, I appreciate your friendship, your seemingly endless passion for our shared heritage and, of course, your willingness to write the foreword for this book. I am truly fortunate to call you a friend.

I want to thank my two test readers and, more importantly, longtime friends, Eileen Whitmore and Tonya Wilson. You both enthusiastically read drafts and provided positive thoughts and helpful feedback. I have always appreciated your friendship and support.

I want to give a special thank-you to J. Banks Smither, Laurie Krill and the team at The History Press. Banks, I appreciate you presenting my ideas to your board, providing suggestions to improve my message and endorsing my idea. I have wanted to tell this story for a long time, and both you and Laurie played pivotal roles in bringing it to life.

Finally, I need to thank my partner in all things, my husband, Glenn. No matter what crazy idea I have or what I want to try, you have always been, and continue to be, my biggest champion. Your unwavering faith in me is astounding. There is never a question in your mind that I can't do something, even when I am questioning myself. You kept me encouraged. There was never a complaint about the constant piles of books on the floor or the hours with my face focused on my laptop. The seemingly endless phone calls, appointments and trips to the library. You were supportive of all of it, and for that I am forever grateful. This book is a testament to your love and support. "Thank you" just doesn't seem like enough. So, I'll just say, "I love you," instead.

In Memoriam

Now nearly all those I loved and did not understand when I was young are dead, but I still reach out to them.
—*Norman Maclean*, A River Runs Through It

Gabriele and Lucia (Di Biasi) Fucetola
Ettore Victor and Rosaria (Di Pasquali) Fieramosca
Santo and Concetta (Zinna) Cammarato
Michele and Angelia (Del Guercio) Palmieri
Pasquale and Rosina "Rose" (Fucetola) Fieramosca
Ettore Victor "Sonny" Fieramosca
Gabriel Anthony "Chubby" and Shirley (Skinner) Fieramosco
"Baby" Anthony Fieramosca
Carolina (Fieramosca) Fiore
Mary (Fieramosca) Spina-Karver
Lucille Ann (Fieramosca) Cammarato
Anthony Bolcato
Patrick Anthony "Patty Boy" Fieramosco
Gabriel James "Billy" and Genevieve "Jay" (Masino) Fucetola
Joseph and Anna (Fieramosca) Ciccone
Leonard and Filomena "Elsie" (Maiorano) Ciccone
Frank and Maria R. (Ciccone) Spino
Ralph Fucetola
Michael Monetti
Gerard "Jerry" and Regina (Fucetola) Masino
Arthur and Florence (Masino) Macioci
Joseph and Lucille (Masino) Porcello
Michael and Gilardino (Fieramosca) Caputo
Pascal "Packy" J. Caputo
Earl Caldwell
Joseph and Julia (Kovacs) Maddalena
Winfred A. and Celia (Maddalena) Van Benschoten
Keith Van Benschoten

Left to right: Pasquale Fieramosca, Rosina (Fucetola) Fieramosca, Genevieve "Jay" (Masino) Fucetola and Patrick "Patty Boy" Fieramosco (*in front*). *Courtesy of Andrea Lyn Cammarato-Van Benschoten*.

INTRODUCTION

"You like to tell true stories, don't you?" he asked, and I answered "Yes, I like to tell stories that are true." Then he asked "After you have finished your true stories sometime, why don't you make up a story and the people to go with it? Only then will you understand what happened and why. It is those we live with and love and should know who elude us."
—*Norman Maclean,* A River Runs Through It

Never forget where you came from.
—*Gabriel Anthony "Chubby" Fieramosco*

If we don't tell our own story, someone else will.

Dennis J. Starr wrote in his 1985 book *The Italians of New Jersey*, "The family history of Italian Americans of New Jersey has been neglected by scholars. There is a lack of histories of the Italian American family at the local level, as well as studies that compare the families of Italian Americans and other ethnic groups."[1]

Well, I am not a scholar, but this project had been under development for a long time, and it is finally ready to emerge and share. I hope this book helps bring attention to the important story of the Italian immigrant experience in Newark, New Jersey—a story that deserves to be told.

Nearly 12 million immigrants arrived in the United States between 1870 and 1900.[2] During the 1820–1924 period, 4.6 million of those immigrants were from Italy. From 1891 to 1915, more Italians entered the United States than immigrants from any other country.[3]

In every census since 1840, New Jersey has been one of the states with the highest proportion of residents born outside the country. For 150 years, New York City has been the nation's most important immigrant port of entry. What has happened in New York City, and to a lesser extent in Philadelphia, has always had a major impact on New Jersey's population and economic development.[4]

In 1860, only 105 Italians lived in New Jersey. By 1900, New Jersey was home to more Italians than any other state in the union with the exception of New York and Pennsylvania. By 1960, New Jersey had surpassed Pennsylvania and became the second-largest home to Italians in the United States after New York.[5]

It's during that time frame the story of my family begins in the United States. My great-grandfather Gabriele Ficetola left behind all that he knew in Calabritto and sailed into the unknown. He settled in Newark in 1888. His future wife, Lucia, immigrated in 1902. They married in 1903 and made their home together on North Seventh Street in the First Ward of Newark. My other set of great-grandparents on my mother's side, Ettore Victor and Rosaria Fieramosca, arrived in 1899 and made their home on Cutler Street, also in the First Ward of Newark. Like many

Immigrants coming up the boardwalk from the barge that has taken them off the steamship company's docks and transported them to Ellis Island. The big building in the background is the newly opened hospital. The ferryboat seen in the middle of the picture ran from New York to Ellis Island. *Landing at Ellis Island. New Jersey New York Ellis Island, 1902. Library of Congress.*

Lucia (Di Biase) Fucetola, born in 1869 in Italy, arrived in the United States in 1902. *Courtesy of Andrea Lyn Cammarato-Van Benschoten.*

Left to right: Rosina (Fucetola) Fieramosca, Pasquale Fieramosca, Mary (Fieramosca) Spina-Karver and Lucille Fieramosca (*in front*) at 308 South Nineteenth Street, Newark. *Courtesy of Andrea Lyn Cammarato-Van Benschoten.*

other immigrants of that time, they could not read or write. What they did do, however, was persevere.

On my father's side, my great-grandfather Santo Cammarato, born in 1877 in Cirome, Sicily, arrived in New York in 1904. His wife, my great-grandmother Concetta, born in Gagliano, Sicily, arrived in the United States in 1907. Their American story began on South Tenth Street in Newark. My other set of great-grandparents on my father's side, Michele and Angelina Palmieri, arrived in the United States from Calabritto and settled on North Tenth Street.

My entire family settled in the First Ward of Newark, an area of less than one square mile.

They all became part of a community that rose to over thirty thousand residents. The First Ward's religious heartbeat was St. Lucy's Church. Its cornerstone was laid in 1891, and the church was a primary source of support for tens of thousands of Italian immigrants and their families when they first arrived and settled in their new homeland.

The Italian community in the Iroundbound section of Newark began around Monroe Street in the mid-1870s, quickly expanded to Ferry Street and continued to grow over the decades. Also known as "Down Neck," the community was in need of its own spiritual center to meet the needs of the Italian immigrant community, so the Dutch Reformed Protestant Church was purchased and transformed into Our Lady of Mount Carmel in 1890.

Additional smaller Italian neighborhoods were settled throughout "Nevarca," as the immigrants called their new home. They brought with them their history and heritage while developing their own traditions. They worked hard to succeed and evolve into what is now referred to as Italian American culture.

What you will find presented here is a mix of data and fact coupled with personal stories and narratives. It is not meant as a rationalization or defense. It is "us" as a community. We are often misunderstood and maligned. We are not the caricatures that are often shown in today's media. Italians in New Jersey were and are a special breed. We have a strong sense of faith, family and, of course, food. We know how to laugh at ourselves, but we aren't afraid to stand up to those who portray us in a poor light. We are the perfect combination of American and heritage. Like my Uncle Chubby always reminded us kids growing up, we as a community have never forgotten our roots.

I hope you come on this journey with me and learn about all the first Italian immigrants to Newark, New Jersey, faced, how they persevered and how I hope we as a community will continue to evolve.

1

THE HISTORY OF THE GREAT MIGRATION, 1880-1920

Before the Italian neighborhoods of Newark became well-established, before the Great Migration, it is important to understand why. Why would millions of people leave the towns and villages where their families lived for generations?

"They Came in Search of a Better Life"

From before the American Revolution to the present day, Italians have been coming to this nation in search of the American dream. There are as many different reasons they came as people who left their homeland

Italian immigrants on the deck of a steamship. *Courtesy of the* Italian Tribune.

for a chance at a new life. While some came for the adventure, many more came to escape continued hardships and poverty after the unification of Italy in 1861.

When a young person asks an elder family member why their ancestors decided to come to America, the standard answer is often the same: "They came in search of a better life." But what does that actually mean? The phrase often conjures nostalgic thoughts of grainy black-and-white photos of immigrants holding American flags, looking up at the Statue of Liberty, waiting for their turn to go through Ellis Island.

In reality, the answer is far more complex, however: most Italian emigration can be traced to Italy's unification. During the period of the Great Migration, 80 percent of the immigrants came from the Mezzogiorno, the provinces south of Rome as well as the island of Sicily.

A History of Occupation

No one has come to this land except as an enemy, a conqueror, or a visitor devoid of understanding….No message, human or divine, has reached this stubborn poverty.
—*Carlo Levi*, Christ Stopped at Eboli: The Story of a Year

The invasions of the entire Italian peninsula after the fall of the Roman Empire further corded the conditions of the south. In the ensuing centuries, first the Arabs, then the Normans, followed by a host of other foreigners, including the Germans, the Spaniards and the French, overran the area in a succession of waves.[6] Repeated invasions by foreign powers left their mark on language, customs and beliefs.[7] The native residents of Italy rarely had control of their own land or their own lives. Corruption was rampant. Heavy tax burdens were sometimes levied on the poor of the south for the sole purpose of appropriating their homes and possessions if they fell behind on tax payments. Forced ignorance was widespread throughout the south, as schools were scarce and primarily reserved for the children of wealthy northerners. As time progressed, however, the idea of "Young Italy" began to develop, and four men steered the way.

During the time of the Congress of Vienna, Italy was divided into eight principalities under Austrian, Bourbon and Papal rule. Only Sardinia and Piedmont were allowed to continue as regions independent of foreign rule. They did not share much, neither a common language nor a country. During this period, a small percentage of the nation spoke what is considered modern-day Italian. The large majority of Italians spoke regional languages, often referred to as dialects by the generations after the initial migration. Italy moved toward unification, but only in name. There was no common identity.

Risorgimento!

What is considered "modern Italy" began in the early nineteenth century with the Risorgimento and was a call for the people to "Rise Again," this time moving toward a unified country with the belief it would lead to a prosperous and independent future. This called for a transition from a feudal system to a capitalist economy and the development of a middle class.[8]

Meanwhile, a small group of men was developing a plan for true Italian unification. Giuseppe Mazzini, King Victor Emmanuel II, Count Camillo Benso di Cavour and Giuseppe Garibaldi looked on this quest as nothing short of a mission from God. Of these four men, it is Garibaldi who is remembered by many of the "Italians" that left their homeland after unification. Garibaldi would eventually be considered almost a folk hero by southerners, as they looked to him as a liberator. The four relied on a past that validated their political demands; they referred to a foul present of foreign oppression, internal divisions and defeat in order to belittle their ruling governments.[9]

Garibaldi was beloved by millions of Europeans, mainly because of his democratic attitude toward persons of all stations, yet he implicitly believed that a dictatorship—with benign motives—was the most effective means of imposing constructive social reforms on a people. "Sometimes," he was quoted as saying, "you have to force liberty on people for their own good."[10]

Throughout Garibaldi's life, he was considered by many to be an idealist and believed in the honesty of others. Unfortunately, far too often, that would prove to be his downfall.

For many who looked at the Risorgimento with an eye to what came after, Italy's history between 1815 and 1870 became a story of broken promises and missed opportunities, which gave rise to a country of regret, corruption and thwarted ambition. The well-to-do northern leaders believed they were creating a revolution for the poor of the south, when in reality, they were making it for themselves.[11]

Giuseppe Garibaldi in Naples, Italy, circa 1861. *Library of Congress.*

Post-Unification

Garibaldi's triumph with Italian unification was considered, according to lectures at Cooper Union Institute, "one of the greatest achievements in military history…by the George Washington of Italy."[12] While unification was being celebrated across the Atlantic, trouble was developing in the south of Italy, as the northern and southern regions of the newly unified country were lacking a unified economy, culture or identity.

The first warning sign of southern Italy's dissatisfaction with the nation's political turmoil took place when King Victor Emmanuel announced unification was complete. Southern Italians were believed to be forever connected to their native homeland. The reports of northern government officials stationed throughout the Mezzogiorno confirmed the general impression of their superiors, notwithstanding the peasant revolts against the reign in the 1860s, that southern Italians were an apathetic lot, hopelessly fatalistic, hardly the sort to stray from what they conceived as their preordained way of life.[13]

The sky was a mixture of rose, green, and violet, the enchanting colors of malaria country, and it seemed far, far away.
—*Carlo Levi*, Christ Stopped at Eboli: The Story of a Year

In Carlo Levi's profound autobiographical novel, *Christ Stopped at Eboli*, the author describes his yearlong exile in a remote village in southern Italy. Levi delves into the lives and abject poverty the peasants of a remote village in Lucania (now Basilicata) endured on a daily basis.

The newly created Kingdom of Italy sold a large amount of land previously owned by the Catholic Church. However, instead of helping improve the lives of the poor by giving residents of the Mezzogiorno the opportunity to purchase property, they were unable to afford the newly available land. As a result, much of the land was purchased by the wealthy or speculators. The new landowners cleared much of the forested areas for agricultural use, resulting in soil erosion and the development of marshes. These marshes became prime breeding grounds for mosquitos carrying malaria. On average, two million people in the Mezzogiorno became infected with malaria each year. As late as 1904, when emigration from Italy was at its peak, approximately twenty thousand Italians died from malaria annually.[14]

Unlike northern and central Italy, where rivers and lakes were plentiful, the south was painfully dry. While the installation of irrigation systems in the south would have improved its economy greatly, the new national government chose to develop irrigation systems only in the north. Drinking water in many small villages was most often collected from rainwater. As late as 1921, only 8 percent of all artificially induced irrigation in Italy was developed in the south.[15]

In reality, Garibaldi and others from the north knew almost nothing about the day-to-day lives of the southern people. He would follow the example of other northerners who had grand ideas on how to improve the lives of southern Italians, yet none of those ideas helped resolve the real problems the southern Italians faced. His attempts, however, endeared him to southern residents, as they looked at him as an individual who fought on their behalf, but Garibaldi failed, leaving them in their impoverished lives. In many ways, the south became worse off after unification.

I was ignorant of the fact that the newly unified state ferociously taxed millions of desperate southerners who emigrated to America to financially support the owners of the ships that carried them and of the northerners, who vacationed for a few months of the year in Switzerland.
—*Pino Aprile,* Terroni

This new unified government proved to be more oppressive than any invader of the previous centuries. Southerners were considered inferior to their northern neighbors, while the northerners considered themselves "modern and enlightened" liberators of a nation. The new Italian state imposed new and higher taxes on the population. The heavy debt from the wars fought to create a unified Italy required repayment.[16] Only 2 percent of the Italian population was qualified to vote at the time, which left the wealthy firmly in control of the new centralized government and therefore able to enact legislation to favor their interests. Northern Italy possessed 48 percent of aggregate wealth and assumed 40 percent of the public debt. Central Italy possessed 25 percent of aggregate wealth and assumed 28 percent of public debt. Southern Italy possessed 27 percent of aggregate wealth and assumed 32 percent of public debt.[17] In order to pay each region's share of the debt, tax decisions were heavy-handed. For example, mules, which were essential to the lowly farm worker, were subject to taxation, but cows—nearly always the property of affluent landowners—were not. Taxes in Italy during this period were the highest in Europe. Excise taxes were placed on salt, sugar, tobacco and liquor.[18]

After King Emmanuel's announcement, Italians began to leave unified Italy in large numbers. The Italians left but not by choice. They left for the literal survival of their families. By the end of the 1870s, an annual average of over 117,000 Italians had left the country. By 1900, approximately 5.3 million Italians had emigrated for foreign lands.[19] By the time Italians began to emigrate, they had developed a deep distrust of politicians and big government, which they carried with them to their new homelands.

> *Do not delude yourselves into thinking that these people are leaving in search of riches. They are leaving in tears, cursing the government and the signori.*
> —*member of the Chamber of Deputies Ercole Lualdi of Lobardi*

Shortly before Garibaldi's death, he was quoted saying, "It is a different Italy than I had dreamed of all my life, not this miserable, poverty-stricken, humiliated Italy we see now, governed by the dregs of the nation."[20]

The hemorrhaging of Italians continued until the U.S. Congress implemented the Emergency Quota Act of 1921 and the Immigration Act of 1924.

Millions of Dreams

In the 1880s, Italian immigrants in the United States numbered 300,000. In the 1890s, that number increased to 600,000. In the decade after that, the total number of Italian immigrants in the United States swelled to more than 2 million. The greatest period of immigration by Italians took place between 1901 and 1910, when over 2 million immigrants landed on the shores of the United States.[21] By 1920, more than 4 million Italians had come to the United States and represented more than 10 percent of the nation's foreign-born population.[22] From 1891 to 1915, more Italians entered the United States than immigrants from any other country.[23]

From 1855 to 1890, most immigrants arrived at Castle Garden Emigrant Depot, located at the southern tip of Manhattan, which served as the New York State immigration station. Beginning in 1892, immigrants began processing through Ellis Island. During the island station's forty-year history, over 12 million immigrants passed through its gates with an average of 5,000 arrivals per day.[24] First- and second-class passengers were not required to undergo the typical inspection process at Ellis Island. Instead, these passengers received a simple inspection onboard their ship. It was believed that if an individual could afford to purchase such a costly ticket, they were less likely to become a public charge in America due to medical or legal reasons.[25] However, steerage passengers would undergo a much more rigorous process.

Steerage passengers traveled in overcrowded and unhealthy conditions on the bottom decks of the ship. They had limited access to the open air outside their assigned space. The trip across the Atlantic would take on average two to three weeks. The passage across the ocean "seemed to have been so calculated," one immigrant recalled, "as to inflict upon us the last, full measure of suffering and indignity, and to impress upon us for the last time that we were the 'wretched refuse' of the earth; to exact from us a final price for the privileges we hoped to enjoy in America."[26]

Once a steerage immigrant arrived on Ellis Island, they were checked for physical and mental fitness to ensure they could find work in the United States. If someone failed an eye exam or was considered too weak for manual labor, they could be sent back to their homeland. Doctors would look for trachoma (a highly contagious infection of the eye), mental deficiency and lameness, as well as a host of other ailments. The goal was to ensure those

Castle Garden, Battery Park, Battery Park. *Library of Congress.*

Italian immigrant family on ferry leaving Ellis Island, 1905. *Library of Congress.*

who were admitted would not become burdens of society. While less than 2 percent of Italians were forced to return to Italy, fear of family separation caused some immigrants to rename Ellis Island L'Isola dell Lagrime—the Island of Tears.[27]

Legacy

In 1907, Jennifer Zarra-Daudelin's grandfather left behind all he knew as a teenager in his little village of Teora in the Province of Avellino for the United States. He was sponsored by his brother-in-law, and after processing at Ellis Island, he settled in Newark.

He worked as a "hot carrier," a construction worker who carried hot tar up to roofs for application. It was certainly not an easy job. What it did give him, however, was an opportunity.

"I am incredibly grateful for the sacrifices that my ancestors made over a hundred years ago," Jennifer shared with me. "I often think about their strength and perseverance to overcome the challenges of coming to a new

U.S. inspectors examining eyes of immigrants, Ellis Island, New York Harbor, circa 1913. *Library of Congress.*

country with little money, needing to learn a new language, and only the promise of a job."

Over time, that job and hard work allowed Jennifer's grandfather to purchase a home in Newark. That is the home where her family would spend their Sundays enjoying dinner together. Like many others I have spoken with, some of her strongest memories growing up focus around the dinner table—family and food: "I would have to say the food, especially the Feast of the Seven Fishes that we always kept on Christmas Eve. Both my mom's and dad's side followed this tradition, and we do to this day."

Jennifer now spends a lot of time conducting genealogy research to learn about her family and heritage so she can pass this important information on to the next generation of her family: "I started doing genealogy research quite a few years ago to learn more about my grandmother, my father's mother, who passed away when my dad was only two years old. During that time, I uncovered so much more information. I've shared the census data, citizenship papers, plus any family stories with my children."

Another common thread among those I chat with is the importance of heritage in daily life and making sure that connection stays relevant, especially as they age.

"It has meant so much more as I've gotten older. My family has been here for a long time and each generation seems to lose a little bit of our heritage," Jennifer shared. Of course, the chat turned to food. "For example, I know that I don't cook or bake in the same way as my first-generation ancestors. However, I want to keep the ties through food and stories to my ancestors. Italians have such a rich history and culture."

Food and family. A constant theme with Italian immigrants and their families. And pride.

"I think they would be proud of their legacy."

I wholeheartedly agree, Jennifer.

Italian Immigrants in New Jersey

While New Jersey in the mid-1800s had a relatively small number of Italian immigrants that called the state home, their numbers grew quickly. By 1880, New Jersey ranked eighth among the states with the most Italians and was home to 3.5 percent of the nation's Italian immigrants. By 1900, more Italians lived in New Jersey than any other state, except New York and Pennsylvania. In 1960, New Jersey moved ahead of Pennsylvania and became the state with the second-largest Italian population, behind New York.[28]

The first U.S. Census to distinguish nationalities was taken in 1850. At that time, 3,645 Italians lived in the entire nation. As immigration progressed, the large majority of Italian immigrants came from the southern region of the country. When they arrived in their new homeland, they elected to maintain Italian culinary habits, consume wine and perpetuate religious and recreational activities.[29]

The 1980 Census was the first in which Americans were asked to identify their ethnic affiliation, regardless of when their ancestors had immigrated. Based on the question, there were 835,277 people of "pure Italian" ancestry and 480,355 people of mixed ancestry (Italian and other groups) in New Jersey. In total, this represented 17.9 percent of the state population.[30]

"NEVARCA"

They heard about America and a place called Nevarca, and so they came to settle and build. They brought with them their language, culture, traditions and religious beliefs, especially their Old World expressions and devotions to the saint for the paese.
—*Reverend Thomas D. Nicastro,* The Feast of St. Gerard Maiella, C.Ss.R.: A Century of Devotion at St. Lucy's, Newark, New Jersey

In 1860, only 105 Italians lived in Newark. Italian immigrants began to cross the Hudson River from New York into Newark in the 1870s, primarily from Campania, Calabria and Sicily. In 1880, Italian immigrants residing in the city numbered 407. Between 1880 and 1910, approximately 20,000

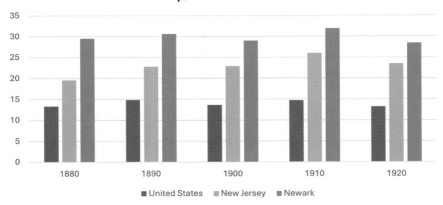

Percentage of foreign-born population in the city of Newark, in the state of New Jersey and in the United States, 1880–1920. Based on data from Historical Census Statistics on the Foreign-Born Population of the United States: 1850–1990.

newcomers were added. By 1920, 27,465 Italians were living in Newark. At the height of Newark's Italian population, Italian Americans had become Newark's largest ethnic group. According to research conducted in 1970, 52 percent of the Italian immigrants and their descendants living in Newark were from Campania.[31] Those of Italian birth and parentage made up 15 percent of the city's population. Italian immigrant colonies established themselves in multiple areas throughout the city, including the Ironbound, Fourteenth Avenue, Silver Lake and the First Ward. Newark provided improved living conditions over the tenements of New York and offered opportunities for work nearby. While a few neighborhoods did not last long, the majority of these enclaves were in place for decades.

An Attempt to Identify Ethnic Neighborhoods

In 1911, Reverend D.W. Lusk (Newark Presbytery), John P. Fox (surveyor) and the New Jersey Bureau of Associated Charities attempted to identify neighborhoods and enclaves by race and ethnicity. The originators of the map estimated the Italian population in Newark in 1911 at fifty thousand, equal to the estimated Jewish population. While some of the areas are somewhat accurately represented, others were either overexaggerated or misclassified, even though the United States conducted a census and the data was easy to access, given the time in history.

Brendan O'Flaherty, PhD, professor at Columbia School of Economics, conducted an analysis of the 1911 map and identified flaws in the neighborhood identification and geography.

Notice that it has no source; it's just what some church people think is going on.…From the 1910 census, I can see some errors in the beloved 1911 map. The most obvious is in the location of the African American population. It correctly shows large numbers of African Americans in the 2nd and 4th wards, but misses the large numbers in the 3rd and 7th wards, especially. The 7th ward had the second largest number of African Americans in 1910, after the 2nd ward. In the Ironbound, it misses the large Irish population of the 5th ward. It also misses the large Italian populations in the 14th and 10th wards. The Chinese presence is exaggerated in the 4th ward. There were 100 persons who were "Indian Chinese and Japanese" in that ward, slightly less than the number of people born in Scotland. And of course, the map doesn't include Vailsburg. I think Newark was much

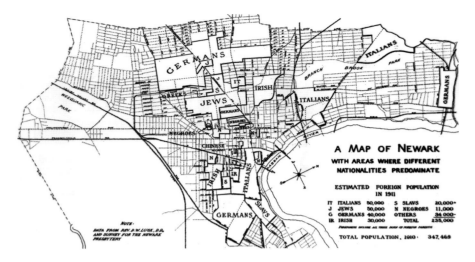

Map of ethnic neighborhoods in Newark in 1911. This was created by Reverend D.W. Lusk, Newark Presbytery; John P. Fox, surveyor; and the New Jersey Bureau of Associated Charities. This map is an estimate of enclaves based on data available at the time. *Courtesy of Charles F. Cummings New Jersey Information Center, Newark Public Library.*

less segregated than this map indicates, but since the manuscript census is available now, there is no sense speculating about that.[32]

While there are inaccuracies in the map, it does identify a growing Italian population that would continue to expand well into the twentieth century.

By 1970, there was a massive shift in the overall population of Italians in Newark as well as their enclaves. The 1970 U.S. Census documented twenty thousand fewer Italians than the preceding census.[33] Changes included the disappearance of the South Orange Avenue Colony, a greater concentration of Italians in the Silver Lake enclave, the destruction of the First Ward enclave, the overall reduction of the Ironbound enclave and the turnover of housing in the Vailsburg area to Italians.[34] Even though the population shifted from Newark to other nearby towns, the families of the original inhabitants of these communities still feel a strong connection to their neighborhoods.

2

DISCRIMINATION AGAINST "I"-TALIANS AND AMERICANIZATION

"The lowest Irish are far above the level of these creatures (Italians)" while the great Emerson rejoiced that the early immigrants brought "the light complexion, the blue eyes of Europe" rather than "the black eyes, the black drop" of southern Europe. Before a congressional committee investigating Chinese Immigration in 1891 a west coast construction boss commented that "You don't call…an Italian a white man…an Italian is a Dago."
—*John Higham,* Strangers in the Land

Italian immigrants, as well as Americans of Italian descent, have faced discrimination and challenges since they took their first steps in this country. From the largest mass lynching in American history in New Orleans in 1891 to a flippant headline using a play on words of a New Jersey politician's last name on Politico[35] in 2022, the fact is discrimination is still taking place and stereotypes are still prevalent. A story I heard regularly while growing up is a perfect example.

When my grandparents moved to their new home many decades ago, they had a non-Italian neighbor. The woman came over to my grandmother and introduced herself. She noted the family's "I"-talian last name and asked if they would be going to "our Church." Without missing a beat, my grandfather came up behind my grandmother and remarked, "I thought it was God's Church."

Italians and other immigrant groups were long the subject of stereotyping by native-born Americans. Pejorative labels such as "dago," "guinea" and "wop" were applied to all Italians regardless of their village or regional origins in Italy that meant so much to the newly arrived immigrants. While some Italians undoubtedly tried to downplay their ethnicity, others developed a greater awareness of it in the face of condescension and hostility.[36]

THE BLACK HAND, THE DAGOES AND POLITICS

"He's a mean son of a bitch."
"I wouldn't be surprised if he didn't have some Mafioso major connections."
"Well, he acts like one."
—*former president Bill Clinton and Gennifer Flowers speaking about Governor Mario Cuomo (secret recording by Flowers, 1991)*

The concept of the Black Hand and the Italian Mafia followed Italian immigrants from their homeland to the United States, and the widely believed stereotype stuck. The first use of the term *Mafia* in news coverage was after the killing of corrupt police chief David Hennessy, when Sicilian immigrants were charged. News reports of the event claimed the chief said, "The Dagoes did it," before he died. When the defendants were acquitted due to lack of evidence, an angry mob broke into the prison to seek retribution for the murdered police chief. At the end of the day, eleven Sicilian immigrants were beaten, shot and hanged, accounting for the largest single mass lynching in American history. Press coverage had an anti-Italian tone, and the lynchings were considered justified.

Monday, we dined at the Camerons; various dago diplomats were present, all much wrought up by the lynching of the Italians in New Orleans. Personally, I think it rather a good thing, and said so.
—*letter from Theodore Roosevelt to his sister Anna Roosevelt*

John Parker, who helped organize the lynch mob, later went on to be governor of Louisiana. In 1911, he said Italians were "just a little worse than the Negro, being if anything filthier in [their] habits, lawless, and treacherous."

Organizations like the Order Sons and Daughters of Italy and the Italian American One Voice Coalition have worked hard to fight back against the negative stereotypes, but they persist even today. Despite these

TRIPLE NUMBER

FORTY-SIXTH YEAR.

DEMONS LOOSE IN NEW ORLEANS

A Wild Mob Numbered by the Thousands Avenges the Murder of Chief Hennessey.

THE WRETCHED SICILIAN BAND BUTCHERED.

Cut Down by a Rain of Lead While They Crouched Like Hunted Animals in Their Prison Yard.

CRAZY POLIZZI TWICE STRUNG UP TO A LAMPPOST.

Scenes Unequaled in Lawlessness and Violence—The Mob Well Managed, but Determined —The Action Deliberately Decided Upon at a Meeting Beneath the Statue of Henry Clay—Speeches Made by the Leaders—Arms, Battering Rams and Ropes All Ready When the Crowd Reached the Prison—No Resistance Offered by the Authorities—A Successful Effort Made to Save All but the Eight Parties—The First Citizens Approve the Deeds of Violence—Action of the Exchanges.

[SPECIAL TELEGRAM TO THE DISPATCH.]

NEW ORLEANS, March 14.—A mob, extraordinary in size, extraordinary in its makeup, extraordinary in its determination, to-day killed 11 of the 19 Italians charged with the murder of Chief of Police Hennes-

and determination, and it was known that if they went down to the Parish prison to take it they would take it at the cost of life.

The Authorities Conveniently Inactive.

The fact that the call had been issued leaked out last night about midnight and was very generally discussed in the bar-

Front-page story from the *Pittsburg Dispatch* on March 15, 1891, reporting the lynching of eleven Italians and Sicilians for their alleged role in the murder of Police Chief David Hennessy after the acquittal of several of the defendants. It was the largest single mass lynching in American history. *Library of Congress.*

unfavorable portrayals and commonly held beliefs, the truth is the majority of Americans of Italian descent and Italian immigrants were historically law-abiding and had no association with the Italian Mafia or organized crime, and this remains the case today.

ATTEMPTS TO SLOW THE ITALIAN TIDE

The U.S. government made repeated attempts in the late nineteenth and early twentieth centuries to stem the tide of Italian immigration. Its first attempt was the development of the Immigration Restriction League in 1894. Founded by three Harvard graduates, the League's focus was to address what the members saw as serious problems in the immigration system and to lobby the U.S. government for immigration reform. They also pushed to gain support for immigration restrictions from major intellectual, industrial and philanthropic individuals and organizations, as well as pass laws effecting the restrictions.[37] This was at the beginning of what is considered the Great Migration for Italian immigrants.[38]

THE 1911 DILLINGHAM IMMIGRATION COMMISSION REPORT

In 1907, the U.S. Congress authorized a high-level joint House-Senate commission to research the causes and impact of recent immigration. The hope was to build support for significant restrictions on southern and eastern European immigration with a focus on Italians, Armenians and Poles. Led by Vermont senator William P. Dillingham, the so-called Dillingham Commission produced a forty-one-volume study in 1911. The study echoed the recommendations of the Immigration Restriction League and urged reducing immigrant numbers by turning away what could be considered "low quality persons."

The Dillingham Commission Report included a "Dictionary of Races and Peoples," which gave descriptions of different ethnicities and their perceived positive and negative traits. The commission offered a specific differentiation between northern Italian immigrants and southern Italian immigrants:

An Italian sociologist, Niceforo, has pointed out that these two ethnic groups differ as radically in psychic characters as they do in physical. He describes the south Italian as excitable, impulsive, highly imaginative, impracticable; as an individualist having little adaptability to highly organized society. The north Italian, on the other hand, is pictured as cool, deliberate, patient, practical, and as capable of great progress in the political and social organization of modern civilization.[39]

The report also noted violent crime was more prevalent in southern Italy, as "secret organizations of the Mafia and Comorra, institutions of great influence among the people, which take the law into their own hands and which are responsible for much of the crime, flourish throughout southern Italy."[40] The report mentions the need to settle wrongs after the fact in the manner of vendetta.

The Dillingham Report also cites the high illiteracy rate and elevated poverty levels and points specifically to Sicily and Calabria as the least productive, most poorly developed portions of the country. These findings fed into the worst fears of the Immigration Restriction League raised during its initial formation in 1894.

The Immigration Act of 1917

Another significant attempt to limit the numbers of southern Europeans, namely Italians, was the Immigration Act of 1917. For the first time, a literacy test was required to gain entry into the United States. Despite President Woodrow Wilson's veto of the act, Congress had the two-thirds vote to override his veto and passed the Immigration Act of 1917. For the Immigration Restriction League, this was a major win, as this had been a critical part of their plan since the organization's inception.[41] According to a study that included literacy data, of the 8,323 communities (June 1919), only 6 were without illiterates and only 13 had less than 1 percent, all of these being situated in northern Italy, and 456 situated in south central and southern Italy had an illiteracy rate of 75 percent and over.[42]

THE 1921 EMERGENCY QUOTA ACT

By far the biggest move to prevent Italians from immigrating to the United States was the Emergency Quota Law in 1921. As fear spread with World War I, Congress and the White House took drastic measures to reduce the flow of immigration. The annual quota for each country of origin was calculated at 3 percent of the total number of foreign-born persons from that country recorded in the 1910 U.S. Census. From 1891 to 1900, 655,694 immigrants came to the United States from Italy. From 1901 to 1910, 2,045,877 immigrated. From 1911 to 1920, 1,109,524 immigrated to the United States. In 1922, only 40,319 were allowed into the United States.[43]

THE JOHNSON-REED ACT

The final nail in the Italian immigration coffin was the Immigration Act of 1924, commonly known as the Johnson-Reed Act. Quota limits per country were again reduced from those established by the 1921 Emergency Quota Act to now just 2 percent of the foreign-born population recorded in the 1890 census. Ethnic groups settled in the United States the longest amount of time—specifically the British, Germans and other northwest Europeans—were assured the largest representation in this new quota system. Meanwhile, more recent immigrant groups, specifically Greeks, Italians and Poles, received the smallest. A new quota took effect in 1927, based on each nationality's share of the total U.S. population in the 1920 census, further reducing the allowable quota for Italian immigrants. This system would stay in effect until 1965. By 1929, the total number of Italian immigrants admitted to the United States was capped at just shy of six thousand; compare this to the United Kingdom, which was capped just shy of sixty-six thousand.[44] Europe was broken down into multiple regions. "Europe" was considered mostly the British Isles: the United Kingdom, Northern Ireland and Ireland. Western Europe included Belgium, Luxembourg, the Netherlands, Austria, France, Germany and Switzerland. Southern Europe included Greece, Italy, Portugal and Spain. As the decades progressed, it was the southern European region that suffered the most stringent overall quotas.

This marked the true end of the Great Migration of Italian immigrants to the United States. While Italians would continue to immigrate, ethnic quotas remained in effect until 1965.

In a paper by Graziano Battistella of the Center for Migration Studies, one of the conclusions determined:

Trends in Italian immigration (small numbers of persons who intend to join relatives and take their chances in America; who are better qualified and better prepared to enter the U.S. labor market and less determined to settle permanently in the United States) lead to some indications for the future of the Italian community in America. The low supply of new immigrants will leave the Italian-born a much-reduced group in the United States, with less influence on the Italian American group in general. Knowledge of Italian language, Italian customs and traditions, survival of Italian culture will become increasingly less common among the group.[45]

The immigration restrictions imposed during the early twentieth century contributed to his findings.

Discrimination continued against the Italian American community from both the government and the general population. The next humiliation and wave of oppression would take place a little more than a decade after the Johnson-Reed Act.

World War II and the Complexities of Italian Ethnicity

"I never heard of any of this."

That was the shocked response from a very well-educated friend as I shared some of what Italian immigrants and Americans of Italian descent endured during World War II. It was an incredibly challenging time for not just Japanese immigrants in America, as we were all diligently taught in school. It was also a challenging time for German and Italian immigrants. Americans of German descent deserve to have their story told. I am here, however, to share the stories of the Italian community here in the United States.

The Italian government began World War II on the wrong side of history. As a result, every Italian immigrant and American of Italian descent would be considered guilty until proven innocent in the eyes of the American establishment. Many members of this community would lose their personal belongings, their property, their businesses and their freedom across the country.

"Do you think that's why your grandmother didn't want you to learn Italian?"

It was a question that gave me pause. I was always taught to be American first while honoring my Italian heritage. "An American of Italian descent"—that's how it was always phrased. Now, as I continue to learn how Italians were treated during World War II, I wonder if this might have had something to do with her continued protests against my learning the language of my heritage. I would put this question to my grandma, but sadly, I am unable to obtain an answer. It is another unanswered question for the ages.

THE "ENEMY'S LANGUAGE"

Posters were created cautioning immigrants not to speak their native language, because it was "the enemy's language." The posters urged them to "speak American," and in response, many stores in Italian neighborhoods hung signs announcing that "No Italian was [to be] spoken."[46]

EXECUTIVE ORDER 9066

In the days following the devastating attack on Pearl Harbor, shock gave way to action. American men were lining up to join the military. Women went to work to support the war effort. Everyone had a role to play.

And on February 19, 1942, President Franklin D. Roosevelt signed Executive Order 9066.

Conduct a simple Internet search regarding EO9066 and the information available, including in the National Archives,[47] and the results will primarily focus on the hardships experienced by Japanese immigrants and Americans of Japanese descent. They do not mention how EO9066 affected Italian and German communities in the United States.

But it did.

While EO9066 did not specifically mention any ethnicity, it gave far-reaching authority to the federal government, the Federal Bureau of Investigation (FBI) and the U.S. military.

This order shall not be construed as modifying or limiting in any way the authority heretofore granted under Executive Order No. 8972, dated December 12, 1941, nor shall it be construed as limiting or modifying the duty and responsibility of the Federal Bureau of Investigation, with

UNITED STATES DEPARTMENT OF JUSTICE

★

NOTICE TO ALIENS OF ENEMY NATIONALITIES

★ The United States Government requires all aliens of German, Italian, or Japanese nationality to apply at post offices nearest to their place of residence for a Certificate of Identification. Applications must be filed between the period February 9 through February 28, 1942. *Go to your postmaster today for printed directions.*

EARL G. HARRISON,
Special Assistant to the Attorney General.

FRANCIS BIDDLE,
Attorney General.

AVVISO

Il Governo degli Stati Uniti ordina a tutti gli stranieri di nazionalità Tedesca, Italiana e Giapponese di fare richiesta all' Ufficio Postale più prossimo al loro luogo di residenza per ottenere un Certificato d'Identità. Le richieste devono essere fatte entro il periodo che decorre tra il 9 Febbraio e il 28 Febbraio, 1942.
Andate oggi dal vostro Capo d'Ufficio Postale (Postmaster) per ricevere le istruzioni scritte.

BEKANNTMACHUNG

Die Regierung der Vereinigten Staaten von Amerika fordert alle Auslaender deutscher, italienischer und japanischer Staatsangehoerigkeit auf, sich auf das ihrem Wohnorte naheliegende Postamt zu begeben, um einen Personalausweis zu beantragen. Das Gesuch muss zwischen dem 9. und 28. Februar 1942 eingereicht werden.
Gehen Sie noch heute zu Ihrem Postmeister und verschaffen Sie sich die gedruckten Vorschriften.

敵國外人注意

日獨伊諸國、國籍ヲ有スル在留外人ハ、近イ郵便局ヲ通ジテ身分證明書ヲ申込ム可シ。二月九日ヨリ二月二十八日マデ、其居所所ニ最モ近イ郵便局ニ行キ、説明書ヲ賴ミ樣、願ヒマス。

Notice from the Department of Justice declaring that all enemy aliens must register at their nearest post offices for a certificate of identification. *National Archives.*

respect to the investigation of alleged acts of sabotage or the duty and responsibility of the Attorney General and the Department of Justice under the Proclamations of December 7 and 8, 1941, prescribing regulations for the conduct and control of alien enemies, except as such duty and responsibility is superseded by the designation of military areas hereunder.[48]

A History without Documentation

So why is it my well-educated friend had never heard of restrictions placed on Italian immigrants? Why is their story not widely known? Truth be told, there is very little documentation about what took place. And many of the individuals and families who were subjected to restrictions and internment prefer not to talk about all they endured. As a result, many believe, incorrectly, that the Japanese immigrant community was the only community subjected to such treatment. The terrible treatment of Japanese immigrants and Americans of Japanese descent was meticulously documented. Almost nothing was officially documented at any level of government regarding the restrictions on or internments of German and Italian immigrants.

Most Italian immigrants affected by restrictions, relocations and internments were in California. One of the most well-known stories of this era of humiliation and violations of civil rights was the confiscation of the fishing boat owned by Giuseppe DiMaggio, the father of Yankees great Joe DiMaggio. In 1942, Giuseppe was labeled an enemy alien and was banned from working in San Francisco's coastal wharf, despite living in the United States for forty years.[49] However, according to a report reviewing the status of the Enemy Alien program, it "has, on the whole worked satisfactorily....The problem of the alien enemy has, so far, been met. The dangerous ones are where they should be; the others have been subjected to irritating, but I think, not too confining restrictions on their normal lives."[50]

While this debate raged between the bureaucrats and the military on how to handle those they deemed enemy aliens, the relocation of Italians and Germans proceeded unrecorded and with little notice two months before the mass internment of Japanese immigrants began.[51] Ultimately, EO9066 called for the compulsory relocation of more than 10,000 Italian Americans and restricted the movements of more than 600,000 Italian Americans nationwide.[52]

"ENEMY ALIENS" IN NEW JERSEY...AND MY FAMILY

While most of these violations against Italians took place on the West Coast, Italian immigrants suffered similar civil rights violations in New Jersey.

While reading about this history, I came to learn a shocking fact. My great-grandmother Concetta (Zinna) Cammarato was required to register as an Alien of Enemy Nationality, as she was not a U.S. citizen. Her son, Anthony, went with her to complete her paperwork, as it appears she was illiterate. Each form was signed with a cross and "witnessed by" her son Anthony. Next to each cross was the notation "her mark."

I discovered her sad story while conducting my ongoing research into my family history. When I found her name in a search of the National Archives immigration database, I was thrilled. I immediately sent away for her file and anxiously awaited a response.

In addition to her initial registration file, another document included that I received was dated several years later when she was investigated again—this time for moving without notifying the Department of Justice's Immigration and Naturalization Service of the planned move.

As I read the documents over and over again, I couldn't even begin to imagine what she must have been feeling. Confusion? Fear? A housewife who couldn't read, couldn't write, had never held a job and a mother of four children being investigated because she came from Italy and wasn't a U.S. citizen at the time of World War II. I stared at the small headshot that

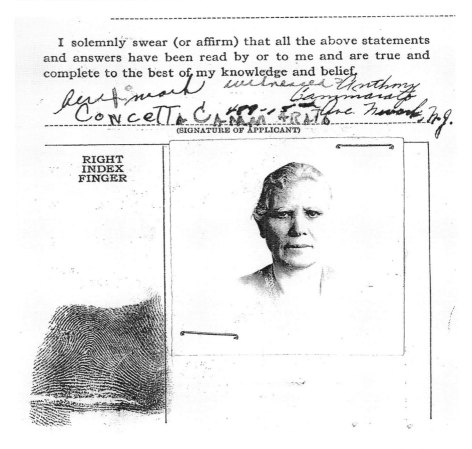

Enemy Alien registration of Concetta (Zinna) Cammarato. The note "her mark" refers to how she signed. All paperwork was witnessed by her son, Anthony Cammarato. *National Archives of Kansas City.*

accompanied the file—it was the first time I had seen a photo of her—and searched for a clue to what was running through her mind. I can see the family resemblance. Her eyes looked sad.

The initial excitement I felt when her name came up in a National Archives search had long since washed away and been replaced with anger and sadness. I thought I was going to receive maybe a copy of her birth certificate or her citizenship documentation. I had no idea this was what I would receive.

I am not certain why she did not become a citizen when my great-grandfather Santo (who had his name Americanized to "Sam") did in 1939. Of the foreign-born living in the United States at the time, 42.5 percent of Italians had not obtained American citizenship when war broke out in December 1941.[53] My speculation is she probably thought that once my great-grandfather was a citizen, it included her as well, as I have read multiple stories from other women of the time who held similar beliefs. Or maybe due to her illiteracy she couldn't become a citizen, as there were literacy and language requirements at various points in history. There was a concern many individuals were waiting to strike the United States from the inside, hence EO9066. History tells us the great attack from within the United States never happened.

Do I think my great-grandmother was a spy waiting to strike at the beginning of World War II? Absolutely not. Her world consisted of her home, her family and her neighborhood in Newark. I found three total change of address forms over the course of her life after her initial registration. She never left Newark. Maybe after her first investigation of failure to register a change of address, she was unable to become a citizen? Sadly, I'll never know. My heart breaks for her.

THE ITALIAN CONTRIBUTION

Despite the persecution they endured, a large number of Italian Americans served in the U.S. military during World War II. Italian Americans rushed to enlist to defend the United States, and more than 1.5 million Italian Americans served in the armed forces during World War II, amounting to some 10 percent of American soldiers in total,[54] more than any other ethnicity to serve in the war.

THE LOSS OF A FIRST WARD SON AND A NEIGHBORHOOD DEDICATION

At 75 Clifton Avenue in the Old First Ward sits the Rotunda Recreation and Wellness Center. In previous decades, it was simply known as the Rotunda Pool, and it is named after a local American hero born to Italian immigrant parents.

Joseph Ralph Rotunda Sr. and his wife, Maria (Stefanelli), had four sons and six daughters. Nine of their ten children were born in the United States. Only the oldest son, Gaetano, known as Gayton, was born in Italy. When World War II broke out, Italian immigrants and their families were eager to prove their loyalty to their newly adopted country and joined the military to fight against their homeland. The boys of the Rotunda family were no different. Gayton served in the U.S. Army and the Marines. Constantine was stationed in Washington, D.C.; John was a first sergeant in the Army and fought in Europe. Joseph Ralph Jr. was a private in the early invasion of North Africa. Sadly, he would lose his life by a land mine while serving his nation with the Cannon Company, 168th Infantry. He was in Tunisia as part of the first wave of invasion of the country. He was

Sign outside Rotunda Pool, later the Rotunda Recreation and Wellness Center. The renaming of the pool took place in 1943. *Courtesy of Andrea Lyn Cammarato-Van Benschoten.*

killed on May 8, 1943, at age twenty-two after serving overseas for only three months.

In 2015, Dr. Michele Rotunda, associate professor of economics, government and history at Union College of New Jersey, and her son, Scott Rotunda Delaney, wrote an extensive history of her great-uncle's sacrifice and the renaming of the pool.

"My grandparents lived on Parker Street in Newark, and we were there at least once a week growing up," Dr. Rotunda shared with me. "My grandfather would always take us everywhere. He would show us the pool and tell us about his brother."

On June 16, 1943, the *Newark Evening News* reported on an announcement from the War Department that included the death of Private Joseph R. Rotunda Jr. as one of four soldiers from New Jersey to lose their lives in combat. The *Italian Tribune* reported Joseph Jr. was identified as the "first American soldier of Italian heritage, from the city of Newark, to be killed in action."

While history would show other Americans of Italian descent from Newark had also been killed in action in May 1943, Ralph Jr. is still documented as the first from the Italian American community in Newark. By the end of the United States' campaign in Northern Africa, a total of eleven service members from New Jersey had lost their lives.

Private Rotunda became a representation of the Italian American community in Newark, the proof they felt was needed to show they were loyal to their new homeland. In October 1943, Ralph Jr. was honored at a memorial service in the First Ward that included a parade in his honor that began at his old high school, Barringer. Additionally, a flag was dedicated that honored First Ward service members. In February 1944, officials from the Veterans of Foreign Wars (VFW) designated the Pvt. Joseph R. Rotunda Jr. Post (No. 848) in honor of the "first soldier from the First Ward to be killed in action in this war." This post became the ninth VFW unit in Newark and enrolled soldiers who were in active service during World War II as well as veterans of World War I.[55] This was a new bit of information Dr. Rotunda learned while she and her son researched the history around her great-uncle's death and how he was memorialized by the community.

The oldest brother, Gayton, was already very prominent in the community and worked with then commissioner Ralph Villani to memorialize Private Rotunda in a larger way. Ralph Villani was commissioner of parks and public property, which afforded him the opportunity to rename Clifton Pool for a fallen Italian American from Newark.

Rotunda Pool, originally known as Clifton Pool, is located at the corner of Clifton and Seventh Avenues. *Courtesy of Andrea Lyn Cammarato-Van Benschoten.*

One month later, the City Commission passed a resolution to rename the Clifton Avenue Pool the Rotunda Pool in honor of Private Joseph R. Rotunda Jr., who was identified as "the first Newark resident of Italian extraction killed in this war." This permanent memorial would ultimately serve as not just a remembrance of Private Rotunda. It would be a long-standing reminder of the service and sacrifice of the Italian American community in the First Ward, as well as other Italian American communities in Newark, during World War II.

"It was a big deal for them that their family fought for the United States," Dr. Rotunda said. "The story was so much about both our Italian heritage and about our American heritage. Both of them were really important whenever I heard the story from my grandfather."

LOYALTY QUESTION ANSWERED

The commitment of these brave young men was proof their allegiance was no longer to Italy but to the United States. The United States now knew Italian immigrants and their families were in fact "American." Despite the sacrifice of this community nationwide, Italian immigrants would suffer humiliation throughout the rest of World War II, including questioning the loyalty of an elderly illiterate woman who moved to a new home within the same neighborhood. Sadly, stereotypes and negative depictions of the Italian American community continue to exist today.

3

THE NEIGHBORHOOD

THE OLD FIRST WARD

Our memory is our most precious ability to recall past events.
Remember those many times we walked with our relatives in process asking
for a favor, hoping for some miracle from this great wonderworker. How many
times did that familiar cart bearing his image come by your house?
What about the many times he blessed you and your loved ones? As we
celebrate one hundred years of faith and devotion, listen carefully as you walk
in procession. Permit yourself to step back in time and feel your parents' and
grandparents' presence, listen to the words and sounds on their lips as they
prayed those beautiful prayers in their native tongue, feel their presence as you
listen to the band play those old familiar pieces as they stop at your house as
he with his eyes lifted toward heaven passes by. Then, when you realize that
you've only stepped back in time in the pages of your mind, "put your arms
around (your brothers and sisters) and give them what you need to give to
(your deceased loved ones)."
—*Reverend Thomas D. Nicastro, VF,* The Feast of St. Gerard Maiella,
C.Ss.R.: A Century of Devotion at St. Lucy's Newark, New Jersey

If there is one Italian enclave that stands out from others in Newark, it is the
Old First Ward, now known as the North Ward. While this neighborhood
grew to tens of thousands, it had humble beginnings.

The first enclave for Italian immigrants began in the early 1870s and
was located on Boyden Street. The founder of the Old First Ward was
Angelo M. Mattia, and he arrived in "Nevarca" in 1873. A Calabrittani,

Mattia accidentally boarded a ferry that took him across the Hudson River. Instead of finding work at the New York City docks, he wound up in New Jersey. He met a few fellow Italians who offered him a job in Newark at a lumberyard.[56]

After a week in Newark, Mattia returned to New York City to share his experience across the river and spoke about the opportunities for work. He then convinced many to join him in Nevarca to build a new life and a new community. Mattia kept a spare room in his home on Boyden Street available to able-bodied Italians who came in search of work. They could stay for two weeks in that spare room for free while first getting settled in their new community.[57]

Over time, more Italian immigrants settled in the area, and the neighborhood expanded to Quarry Street and Drift Street. This continued to develop into the Old First Ward, the largest Little Italy in New Jersey and fifth largest in the United States.

In 1880, just over four hundred Italian immigrants were living in Newark, and they provided cheap labor to a rapidly growing city. They dug ditches, laid railroad tracks and began work on the newly created Branch Brook Park, designed by Frederick Law Olmsted and Calvert Vaux. The city was moving into the modern era on the backs of these immigrants.

THE CREATION OF A COMMUNITY

Eighth Avenue, the enclave's main thoroughfare, and Seventh Avenue, from Stone Street to Garside Street, were lined with pushcart peddlers, barkers, and vendors, calling out their wares, straining to be heard above the din of competing voices.
—*Michael Immerso,* Newark's Little Italy: The Vanished First Ward

Members of the continually expanding community of the Old First Ward brought their culture with them from their small towns in southern Italy. A movie theater on Seventh Avenue and a traditional marionette theater, also on Seventh Avenue, staged elaborate productions with two-foot-tall puppets.[58] Children played in the streets. It was their own bustling world.

Boys playing on Mount Prospect Avenue, circa 1945. *Courtesy of Annette Zarra CiFalino of Nutley; Gerard Zanfini and Michael D. Immerso First Ward Italian collection; Charles F. Cummings New Jersey Information Center, Newark Public Library.*

MEMORIES AND TRADITION

In 1907, Salvatore Petriello, the great-grandfather of Anne Bosworth, arrived in Ellis Island from Montella, in the province of Avellino, in the region of Campania. He settled in the Old First Ward and began his life in America as a bricklayer. His wife, Generosa, joined him a little more than a year later. Even though both great-grandparents passed away before Anne was born, she heard the stories from her grandmother Carolina growing up.

"My grandmother would tell me stories about how her father fell in love with her mother when he saw her riding into their little Italian town on a donkey," Anne shared. "I was also regularly told about Bisnonna Generosa's healing and spiritual activities as a Janara in Montella, which was often misunderstood and considered witchcraft."

Like many I have interviewed, Anne grew up in a multigenerational household. Spending all that time with her grandmother gave her a unique perspective on day-to-day life. Anne credits her close-knit, and close-by, Italian immigrant family as a source of care and strength anytime she needed extra support.

"I think living so tightly tucked into my family gave me a sense of stability and resilience," Anne shared.

She has worked hard to preserve her Italian heritage and share it with the next generation of her family, and while her daughter has a multiethnic background, she considers her Italian heritage her primary identity. Anne has vowed to learn more about the heritage she cherishes.

"I have always shared everything I knew about our Italian roots and traditions. My daughter is only 25 percent Italian, but she takes that as her full identity. I am currently involved in an extended genealogy project on Ancestry that has helped me reconnect with cousins and learn that our Petriello line goes back many generations in Montella," Anne said. "I am also connected to several Italian American groups and have been re-engaged with learning and speaking Italian with a plan to learn Neapolitan."

Anne Bosworth's grandmother Carolina Petriello-Tasco, who settled in the Old First Ward, circa 1932. *Courtesy of Anne Bosworth.*

Anne cherishes every part of her ethnicity and heritage, as well as what it has taught her and the values she has learned as an American of Italian descent.

"I'm so proud to come from resilient, talented and tenacious people who came here and worked hard to establish a family rich in blessings in a country rich in opportunity," Anne shared. "I also feel great joy in knowing that my family's Italian culture has been responsible for developing the best food in the world and a habit of tremendous hospitality where that food, our language, our culture, our history and our faith have been shared over and over again."

She is reminded of all this heritage and pride every time she wears her great-grandmother's wedding band. I also wear my grandmother's wedding band. I understand the bond all too well. It provides a tangible connection to those who are no longer with us.

"Honestly, it means everything to me," Anne said.

I completely agree, Anne.

"Put That in the Book"

An important resource throughout my research was Michael Immerso's *Newark's Little Italy: The Vanished First Ward*. His book was published in 1997 and was the first work that told the story of the fifth-largest Little Italy in the country.

Like many of the children of the original residents of the First Ward, he heard stories about growing up in the neighborhood: the feasts, the clubs, the restaurants and, of course, the church. Yet there was never an attempt to document the history of it all. He told me when stories were told around the table during Sunday dinner, his uncle, his mother's brother, would say, "Put that in the book." Michael's response was always, "What book?" He hadn't planned on writing a book, but his uncle already knew his nephew would take on this incredible challenge. As time passed, he started to think about the idea—to document the stories and places we all hold so dear in our hearts. What started out as a possible short history of his family turned into a massive undertaking of photo collection, research and narrative documentation from the First Ward's original residents. And boy, are we glad he did.

His connection to the Old First Ward is Garside Street, where both sides of his family settled. While some sections of his family originally settled in New York, they all eventually made their way to the First Ward. Michael's family is part of an additional interesting lineage I had never heard of before our chat. His mother's side of the family is Gaggi (Italian Albanian).

"Around the time of Columbus, Turkey was overrunning Albania, and they fought off the Turks for many years. And when the Albanian leader, Gjergj Kastrioti, died, his supporters fought for another year or two and then they were overrun," Michael explained. "Many of them left Albania and settled in Italy. For five hundred years, they were literally Albanian Italians. They spoke Italian, but their primary language was Albanian and they lived in the villages in the south of Italy."

Just more proof of why Michael's uncle was right—he needed to document this information and write these stories.

"My mother's family and my father's family were living two doors down from each other on Garside Street," Michael shared. "So, they were not yet knowing that these people were all going to be part of the same family through marriage.…At one point, around the 1930s, they were living in households that spanned four generations. My great-grandparents, my grandparents, my parents and then our generation."

As I listened to Michael explain his family history, I was reminded of all the stories we had all heard growing up with similar themes. Close-knit, large families and multiple generations in the same household make perfect sense to us, but to a younger individual or someone outside the community, this could all possibly sound quite strange.

When the Old First Ward was decimated by urban renewal, Michael's family re-created the multigenerational housing plan they had on Garside Street. This time, however, it was on Roseville Avenue and Clifton Avenue.

"My grandfather on my father's side managed to raise enough money to buy a six-unit apartment building in the Roseville Section, so in that household, five of the apartments were his family. They recreated the multigenerational family enclave," Michael said. "My mother and my aunt decided to buy a house together on Clifton Avenue. That was always my aunt's dream. If you lived in the First Ward and wanted to be middle class, you moved up to Clifton Avenue to the Forest Hills section."

Michael Immerso's mother and her cousins on Easter Sunday 1936 on Garside Street in Newark's Little Italy. The four cousins are, *clockwise from bottom left*: Florence Conforti, Maria Zanfini (my mother), Lucy Conforti and Maria Conforti. *Courtesy of Michael Immerso.*

After his aunt saw her "dream house," she realized it was too big for just her and her husband. Michael's mother had just wed, so his aunt suggested they move into the Clifton Avenue house. So, another family enclave was created.

The uncle who urged Michael to "write the book" got married and moved to Belleville, but that wasn't far away at all, as meals were always shared.

"They might well have been living with us on Clifton Avenue since every Sunday, we had dinner together. Every Friday night, they were there," Michael said. "The ten people living in the house were always augmented by four more."

So, when friends suggested moving into an apartment as a group, he told them, "I grew up with an extended family. I'm comfortable with this. I'm comfortable."

"A Magical Place"

When interviewing individuals with a lineage to the Old First Ward, I discovered it is not just what they say. It is where they go. You can see it on their faces as they look off into the distance. You can see them transport themselves to their memories. And for Bob Cascella, curator of the Museum of the Old First Ward and a founding member of the Newark First Ward Heritage and Cultural Society, he can only describe it as "magical."

"It was a magical place. It was a place where on the block you lived was a world. Your family were family. Your friends were family. Even some of your enemies later became family," Bob explained. "The block was cleaned by the mothers; they used to sweep in front of their stoops, and it's a stoop. It's a back porch and a front stoop. But your people were there. You had the 'mom and pop' grocery stores, you used to go in there and they had everything you needed, and they knew you. It's something that they don't have today."

The Italian immigrant enclave that developed over the decades eventually provided everything that was needed by the community. Whether it was the pushcart peddler with baskets of bread or fresh produce for sale down the street, there was very little reason to go outside the neighborhood. It was a single cohesive unit. When Bob compares growing up in the First Ward to today's suburban neighborhoods, there's very little comparison.

"When my kids went to school, there were kids from all over. There was no harmony. Our schools were tight. We were together. When we went to school, we were all together. We hung out on the playground; we hung out on the street corners," Bob shared. "Everything was close. People looked out for you too."

Bob attended Newark High, now known as Barringer, named for the superintendent of schools for Newark during the turn of the century. The high school is the third oldest in the United States.

"When we sing our alma mater, it says 'Newark High,'" Bob told me.

Bob grew up on Mount Prospect Avenue and lived in the neighborhood until 1966. Others weren't so lucky.

ERASED BY URBAN RENEWAL

They didn't walk away from their neighborhood; they were thrown out.
—*Monsignor Granato*

While many people believe the "white flight" after the riots of the late '60s is what caused the Italian population of the First Ward to leave, that isn't completely accurate. It wasn't so much a flight as it was an eviction.

When the soldiers returned to their neighborhood after World War II, there was renewed life and happiness on the streets. New businesses were opening, and the feasts were more elaborate than ever before. However, a change started to take place. The original tenements, which lacked private bathrooms, hot water and central heating, were starting to show their age. Some of the men returning from war were getting married and looking for their own homes.

At the same time, urban renewal was on the horizon in Newark, and its target was the First Ward.

> *Urban planners had begun to envision large-scale federally funded urban redevelopment projects to restore blighted city neighborhoods....First Warders were shocked by the announcement in January 1952 that a large tract in the heart of the neighborhood had been selected for urban renewal.*
> —*Michael Immerso,* Newark's Little Italy: The Vanished First Ward

The headline "Big Newark Slum to Be Housing Site" announced the plan in the *New York Times* in June 1952. It labeled the $40 million urban renewal plan "the largest slum clearance and development project in New Jersey."[59]

In total, 477 acres were cleared for the plan, which included the Columbus Homes and the more upscale Colonnade apartments. Eighth Avenue was replaced with Route 280, which split the First Ward in two. Approximately 1,300 families—4,600 people—were displaced.

When residents of the Old First Ward are asked about what happened in the early '50s, it is as if they are talking about an event that just happened. There is still a lot of anger and sadness.

"Urban Renewal, Which Became Urban Destruction"

Bob Cascella found the perfect way to describe what happened to this bustling immigrant neighborhood. The term at the time was "urban renewal," but there wasn't anything that came from it that could be considered close to renewal.

"Suppose they never had the projects. But those neighborhoods like our neighborhoods, give them loans, put trees up, tell them to redo your house on the outside so you have something nice," was Bob's vision. "If we put something up, the building is going to be two stories, it's going to be nice."

Newark was, in fact, guilty of evicting more people than it accommodated in public housing. Between 1959 and 1967, 3,760 units were built. At the same time, approximately twelve thousand families were pushed out of their homes to make way for public housing, highway and other urban renewal development.[60] In total, 15 percent of the residents of the First Ward left Newark for other towns and never came back. But something completely different happened.

Bob asserted, "They were just told they have to leave. That's what Father said. But they told him. Look, this is it, you have no alternative. Leave or else."

The "Father" Bob referred to was Reverend Gaetano Ruggiero, pastor of St. Lucy's in the 1950s. Father Ruggiero supported the project initially. His successor, Monsignor Joseph Granato, believes Father Ruggiero did not grasp the scale of the project until it was too late.[61]

Father Ruggiero believed it would be good for the people of the community. Several people I interviewed told me Father Ruggiero was destroyed when he saw people of the neighborhood forced out of their homes against their will. He didn't have a restful night's sleep for years.

"The older people didn't want to leave the neighborhoods they had. The houses were nice. They kept the sidewalks clean, like my mother used to do," Bob said. "Newark was a good city. It was a nice neighborhood. All neighborhoods. But they ruined it all."

Some who protested evictions became legendary, like the old woman who swung a lead pipe at policemen as they coaxed her into vacating her bakery on Christmas Eve.[62]

St. Lucy's and Rotunda Recreation and Wellness Center are the only remaining large physical locations that serve as proof there was once a thriving Italian American community in the First Ward.

Surveying the site for Columbus Homes Housing Project in 1953. St. Lucy's Church can be seen in the distance. *Courtesy of Gerard Zanfini and Michael D. Immerso First Ward Italian collection; Charles F. Cummings New Jersey Information Center, Newark Public Library.*

The Christopher Columbus Homes complex was composed of eight twelve-story-tall slabs with two hundred apartments each and followed a typical public housing formula: bare brick on the outside and basic furnishing on the inside. It officially opened in August 1955. Very few of the displaced families returned and lived in the newly opened complex.

The Beginning of the End

Once the evictions began, it marked the beginning of the end of the Old First Ward. The community never rebounded or returned to its former glory. Many blame politicians on the local and state level for what happened. Mayor Ralph Villani and former First Warder Peter Rodino tried to convince the masses this was the right move for the neighborhood and the city.

"Thanks to our politicians like Mayor Villani and Congressman Rodino, we got the Christopher Columbus projects and 280," Bob told me. "Father wrote everyone and said, 'If you stay, we'll stay.' And we did."

St. Lucy's and the Feast of St. Gerard continued to push forward during what some former First Ward residents refer to as the "dark years," which included the destruction of the neighborhood, the development of Route 280 and the Columbus Homes and the Newark riots.

> *Even though many familiar things were changing and collapsing, the one that remained unchanged and timeless in the old neighborhood was and is St. Lucy's and the Feast of St. Gerard.*
> —*Reverend Thomas D. Nicastro,* The Feast of St. Gerard Maiella, C.Ss.R.: A Century of Devotion at St. Lucy's, Newark, New Jersey

Demolition of area of the First Ward along Seventh Avenue in 1953. *Courtesy of Gerard Zanfini and Michael D. Immerso First Ward Italian collection; Charles F. Cummings New Jersey Information Center, Newark Public Library.*

Procession during Feast of Saint Gerard, circa 1960, with Columbus Homes in background. *Courtesy of Gerard Zanfini and Michael D. Immerso First Ward Italian collection; Charles F. Cummings New Jersey Information Center, Newark Public Library.*

When the Columbus Homes was finally closed and demolished in 1994, former residents came to watch the implosion.

"They all cheered," Bob told me.

The congregation was thankful they were able to secure the property in front of St. Lucy's to build St. Gerard Plaza and ensured nothing would ever be built on that space again. It became part of the church property in 1999, exactly one hundred years after the first official Feast of St. Gerard. And Bob credits two Newark politicians for providing key support for acquiring the property.

"We were fortunate because we got the plaza and that was thanks to two people," Bob shared. "Mayor Sharpe James and his aide Calvin West. They liked St. Lucy's. They liked Father Granato. Thanks to them we got that property."

We're Still Here

Just as Michael Immerso's uncle, the storyteller of his family, inspired him to document the history of the Old First Ward, it became even more pressing as the older generations began to pass away.

"Their lives were so entwined with this neighborhood. These are the people who know the stories. So, you either lose the stories or you write down the stories," Michael shared. "I went to the library and there was basically nothing. This is a neighborhood that was erased by urban renewal, and nobody had bothered to document it. Once this generation passes, their memories go."

It was this sense of urgency that pushed Michael to document the history of this "magical place," as Bob Cascella put it. We all owe a debt of gratitude to Michael for his time and research and to his uncle, for first planning the seed of an idea with him. And we owe a debt of gratitude to Bob Cascella, for creating the Museum of the Old First Ward, where the tangible memories of this once thriving neighborhood are kept. It is located in the basement of St. Lucy's Community Center. Considering we were the original "basement Catholics," it seems strangely fitting.

St. Gerard Plaza, outside St. Lucy's Church during the 2023 Feast of St. Gerard. Many families of the original First Ward residents had their loved ones' names inscribed in different locations throughout the plaza. *Courtesy of Andrea Lyn Cammarato-Van Benschoten.*

Domenico Miano looks out from his cousin's ice cream truck. Domenico immigrated to Newark in 1910 at the age of seventeen from Ariano Irpino, Avellino. *Courtesy of the Very Reverend Cav. Thomas D. Nicastro, VF.*

While the neighborhood of Old First Ward has vanished, the children, grandchildren and great-grandchildren of those original residents still return to St. Lucy's every October and remember. Just as Monsignor Granato wrote to his congregants, asking them to stay during the "dark days" of the Columbus Homes, we all continue to stay. And I hope that continues long into the future. We need to remind everyone "we're still here."

> *The generation that grew up in the First Ward in those bygone days holds memories of sights, sounds, and smells that have not faded with the passage of time—the sound of horses' hooves on the ice-clogged cobblestones on Seventh Avenue, the call of the peddlers—"U Trippaiole!" and "U Pizzaiole!"—the smell of chocolate from the Brewster Chocolate Factory on Sheffield street, and of wine during the wine-making seasons when grape crates were piled up high along the curbside.*
> —*Michael Immerso,* Newark's Little Italy: The Vanished First Ward

4
THE NEIGHBORHOOD

THE IRONBOUND/DOWN NECK

The Ironbound neighborhood, also known as Down Neck, began on Monroe Street during the mid-1870s. Its two different nicknames originate from two very different sources. The initial name, Dutch Neck, originated in the 1780s. "Dutch" refers to the national origin of the early Dutch settlers who founded the community in the mid-1700s, and "Neck" likely references the territory itself. Over time, Dutch changed to Down. The Ironbound nickname evolved in the 1830s from the development of the railroads and tracks that surrounded the area. Some have suggested the nickname may be related to the nineteenth-century forges and steel plants, but stronger evidence points to the expanding railroads, as Penn Station was ultimately developed in the area and is now a major hub for train service. Little did those early Italian immigrants in the Ironbound know the Pennsylvania Railroad would disrupt their community multiple times.

WAVES OF IMMIGRATION

And in that same year of 1889, the growing Italian presence on the other side of the tracks—the east side—was marked by the founding of Our Lady of Mount Carmel parish to serve the spiritual needs of that immigrant group's predominately Catholic fold.
—*Edward A. Jardim,* The Ironbound: An Illustrated History of Newark's "Down Neck"

As the English and Irish began to create settlements in the area, Down Neck was still considered an isolated and marshy meadow in the early 1800s. Newark wasn't considered a full-fledged city until 1836. The neighborhood's famous Ferry Street was initially authorized as "Ferry Road" by the 1765 New Jersey legislature.[63] The route was first laid out in the early eighteenth century using logs. In 1849, the logs were replaced by smooth wooden planks and expanded to a new system renamed Plank Road.[64]

By 1830, Newark was home to about ten thousand residents, the majority of which were Irish immigrants. During the same period, a large wave of German immigrants began to arrive in the area. By 1865, one-third of Newark's population was made up of Germans. By the late 1880s, the Italians had begun to make their mark on Down Neck.

Initially, Italian immigrants settled in the area of River and Mulberry Streets. However, the early settlement did not last long. In May 1902, Italian immigrants living in the area were quickly forced to leave after the property was purchased for expansion of the Pennsylvania Railroad. Now in search of a new neighborhood, many moved a few blocks over to the Ferry Street area. The Ironbound enclave continued to grow for well over half a century.

Originally settled by immigrants from Spilinga, a municipality in the Italian region of Calabria, the Ironbound became home to a large and vibrant Italian enclave. The community began on Monroe Street in the mid-1870s and grew rapidly. Its center began to move to Ferry Street, and in 1890, the Old Dutch Reformed Church was purchased and became Our Lady of Mount Carmel Roman Catholic Church to accommodate the needs of this rapidly developing neighborhood. The sale of the Protestant church was symbolic of the German population moving out of the area as Italian immigrant families continued to move in and create their own community. The community continued to expand and settle in the area around Independence Park (originally known as East Side Park).

BOUGHT THE LOTS.

Real Estate Deal Which Was the Outcome of Some Anxiety.

Purchase has been effected by the executors of the estate of the late John O'Brien, who left a considerable amount of property in the Tenth and Fifth wards, of a piece of land containing two building lots, on Elm street near Van Buren street. David Bramley, the local representative of the heirs, acted as the agent. The seller of the lots was Frank Lafalce, who several months ago bought them from the O'Brien estate through a New York agent.

Incidental to the transaction, it is claimed that Lafalce has been a considerable gainer. After he bought the lots, Lafalce had plans drawn for a four-story brick structure to be erected on the lots. Rumor had it that some of the families in the Italian section of River street, who were forced to move on June 1 because of a railroad improvement where they lived, would occupy the apartments.

Adjoining the lots which Lafalce bought are two owned by Max Hillert. He was about

An article from the Newark Evening News on June 17, 1902, announcing additional property purchased for the Pennsylvania Railroad expansion. From the Newark Evening News, June 17, 1902.

In an effort to continue to accommodate the ever-expanding Italian population, the new Our Lady of Mount Carmel Church opened to worshippers in 1955 and rose to become the heartbeat of the Ironbound enclave.

MULTIFAMILY HOMES AND AN ENCLAVE WITHIN AN ENCLAVE

Like many who have their family history in Newark, Carla Conte-Andrews attributes her family's beginnings to the First Ward and the Ironbound.

Carla's mother, Louise Marie Rispoli-Conte, grew up in the Ironbound, and her parents were married in Our Lady of Mount Carmel.

"My mother was born and raised in only one house in the Ironbound," Carla shared. "It was the house next door to my great-grandmother."

Her grandfather Luciano Rispoli grew up on the opposite side of the same Italian enclave in the Ironbound.

The family stayed close physically and emotionally. Her grandmother grew up and stayed in the same house for her entire life. Like many in the tight-knit community, it was a multigenerational home with extended family members all under the same roof. As other relatives aged, they would pool their money and purchase a home as close as next door, creating their own mini family enclave.

"I'm one of those families where everyone was always together until my parent's generation started spreading out farther, all the way to Belleville," Carla joked.

I understand all too well, Carla.

THE ATTEMPTED "AMERICANIZATION" OF IMMIGRANTS

In the early days of the expansion of Newark, street names were often changed to reflect shifts in local and American history. Just as other immigrant neighborhoods were struggling to become "American" in the eyes of native-born Newark residents, a name change took place within the Ironbound. In 1923, East Side Park was renamed Independence Park. Activists within the community had petitioned the Essex County Park Commission to make the change for the purpose of instilling in foreign-born residents "a new significance" about the tenets of democracy. The name change took effect, symbolically, on July 4.[65] This was meant to serve as a constant reminder that these immigrants were in America now and were expected to conform to their new home.

GETTING TO WORK

In the years following 1880 such groups of workers became a familiar sight throughout the city and its environs. Endlessly, it seemed, they swung picks and wielded shovels in the hot sun....This was the price which Newark exacted as an entrance fee from its early Italians who resignedly, sometimes joyfully, accepted menial tasks.
—*Charles W. Churchill,* The Italians of Newark

Despite the eviction of the Italian colony in the area of River Street due to the expansion of the Pennsylvania Railroad, many Italian immigrants went to work on that project.

A Department of Labor Italian class receiving instructions in English and citizenship in an effort to become "American," circa 1920, Newark, New Jersey. *Library of Congress.*

Manual labor was the lot of Newark's first Italians. To them was given the difficult, dangerous work of laying the structural basis of Newark's industrial development. Railroads, transit companies and municipal engineering departments were the first agencies to absorb Italian labor en masse, often following the padrone system.[66]

Promises and the Padrone

The padrone system was a contract labor system that connected Italian immigrants with employers in the United States. The word *padrone* is Italian for "boss," "manager" or "owner." Padrones could be first- or second-generation Italian Americans or individuals still in Italy who would act as middlemen between immigrants and potential employers, collecting a commission from the immigrants for their services.[67]

Padrones often promised young men in Italy employment opportunities, safe passage and housing. The lack of understanding by the potential immigrant of how to gain employment once in the United States worked to the padrone's advantage. In reality, many padrones acted more like slaveholders than managers, controlling the immigrants' wages, contracts and often even food.

The practice of indenturing young children was common in southern Europe, and the padrone system involved recruiting and indenturing the children of the rural Italian poor.

In an effort to prevent the manipulation of Italian immigration, the U.S. Congress, under its power to enforce the Thirteenth Amendment, enacted the Padrone Act of 1874, historically referred to as "Italian Freedom Day" or "J23," in reference to June 23, 1874, the day the act was passed. It was created as a direct response to the exploitation of Italian immigrants and children. It criminalized the practice of enslaving, buying, selling or holding someone in involuntary servitude, including bringing someone into the United States by force or deception with the intent of holding them in confinement or involuntary service.

While employers and middlemen attempted to sidestep the new statute, there were official protections put in place for the recently arrived Italian immigrants.

A STORY OF RESILIENCE

While researching this project, I received the following letter from Maria Somma Dininno. I was moved by Maria's memories and family story:

> *I was watching the news one morning and the mention of the Robert Treat Hotel brought back cherished memories of my parents' wedding on September 24, 1951, at Our Lady of Mt. Carmel Roman Catholic Church on Ferry Street. They began their journey as husband and wife with their first night spent at the Robert Treat Hotel before leaving the next day for their honeymoon to Canada. I was moved to research into the history of the hotel, leading me to your article about Italians who settled in Newark, N.J. I was glad to learn that you are currently working on a book and actively seeking stories and photos of Italian immigrants in Newark. I have a touching family story that I have heard countless times from my father and aunts. I am sure it would be a valuable addition to your collection.*
>
> *My paternal grandmother arrived in the United States at the age of 15, married my grandfather, and faced the challenges of raising 10*

Maria Somma-Dininno's paternal grandmother and her ten children; the young boy is Maria's father. Her paternal grandfather passed away when her father was just two years old. *Courtesy of Maria Somma-Dininno.*

children—nine girls and one boy, my father. Sadly, my grandfather passed away when my father was only 2 years old, leaving my grandmother to cope with the difficulties of life without the support of social security or welfare during the Depression. My family lived in a small cold-water flat on Oliver Street in the Iron Bound area of Newark. To make ends meet, my older aunts sought employment to contribute to the family's finances and cover the rent. An amusing twist emerged each time the landlord visited to collect rent—five children would hide, while the other five remained with my grandmother. The landlord, puzzled by the ever-changing faces, eventually caught on. Gratefully, he recognized the Somma Family as a quiet, clean, hardworking, and faith-filled household, allowing my grandmother, aunts and my Dad to continue residing there.

I believe this story sums up the resilience, unity, and spirit of Italian immigrants in Newark during challenging times. I am eager to share this life story.

As Maria so eloquently shared, every immigrant arrived prepared to work hard and build a family.

MOVING OUT

While Our Lady of Mount Carmel still serves the religious needs of the community, the Ironbound is now dominated by the Portuguese, instead of Italians. A mass is still said weekly in Italian, and the Spilingese Social Club is still situated a few doors down from the church, welcoming Italian members after church. The neighborhood may be a different ethnic community, but you can still find important pieces of the original Italian enclave. You just need to look.

5

THE NEIGHBORHOOD

OTHER ITALIAN IMMIGRANT COMMUNITIES IN NEWARK

While the Old First Ward and the Ironbound were the largest—and longest-lasting—Italian immigrant communities in Newark, there were other enclaves that may have been smaller but were no less important. Some lasted for a short period of time, while others lasted for decades. As the Italian immigrant population began to rapidly grow in the 1880s, Italian immigrants were settled in a variety of different areas throughout the city.

BANK STREET ENCLAVE

The first Italian immigrant community in Newark was located on Bank Street. Unlike areas filled with the throngs of southern Italian immigrants that would follow, the Bank Street enclave was made up of northern Italians, near what would become the Essex County Courthouse. This community would become home to Newark's first Italian Roman Catholic Church, St. Philip Neri. This community was short-lived, however, due to its initial remote location in the city, as well as construction of the Essex County Courthouse complex. By 1942, St. Philip Neri Church was down to five hundred parishioners.

RIVER STREET ENCLAVE

Italian immigrants who settled in what would become the First Ward expanded into the River Street area. However, this was also a short-lived community, as it was "cleared" of Italians in 1902 when the land was acquired for the expansion of the Pennsylvania Railroad.[68]

The proposed project was well documented by the *Newark Evening News* as the Italian enclave worked to save their neighborhood. An article in the May 31, 1902 issue of the *Newark Evening News* reported on an "Exodus from River Street: Italians Moving to Make Room for a Freight Yard." The article reported on the scene as residents moved to other areas of the city.

It was a conglomerate mass of humanity swarmed down River Street toward Ferry Street. The Italian colonies in Jackson and Adams Streets got most of those who moved, although there were some who turned their faces to Drift and other streets in the Fifteenth Ward.
—Newark Evening News, *May 31, 1902*

RIVER STREET WILL HAVE MOVING DAY

Italians Obliged to Migrate Because Tenements Have Been Bought by the Pennsylvania.

TO MAKE A LARGE FREIGHT YARD

The Thickly Populated Structures Will Be Torn Down Within a Short Time and More Facilities Made for the Handling of Trains — Notices Have Been Served on the Tenants that They Must Vacate by June 1.

Where the Italian colony, at present located along River street, will migrate to on June 1 is the subject of much con-

Headline from the *Newark Evening News* on May 7, 1902, reporting on the planned expansion, and ultimate eviction, of the Italian enclave on River Street by the Pennsylvania railroad. *From the* Newark Evening News, *May 7, 1902.*

Another article by the *Newark Evening News* one month later reported that land acquisition continued. The Pennsylvania Railroad Company "wants to acquire all the property on the east side of the tracks between the junction and the Centre Street Station, for a great freight yard."[69]

Fourteenth Avenue

While smaller in geography and population than the First Ward and the Ironbound, the Fourteenth Avenue Italian immigrant enclave was still large enough to develop a thriving community. Historically, this community has been referred to the Fourteenth Avenue enclave, as well as the South Orange Avenue enclave. The entire Italian community was approximately six blocks square. By 1899, there were sufficient numbers of residents to establish the third Italian Roman Catholic Church: St. Rocco's Roman Catholic Church. This neighborhood had a larger population of Sicilians than other enclaves around the city.

In March 1900, the neighborhood was the site of one of the most heartbreaking events in Newark's history. A tenement fire on Morris and Fourteenth Avenues claimed fifteen lives. The fire made national news. One of the saddest reports was from the *New York Times* of March 13, 1900: "Mrs. Casillo was found with two of her children clasped in her arms. The little fellow Frank had his face buried in her breast, while the baby was thrust beneath her night gown to save it from the smoke."

FOURTEEN DEAD IN A BURNING TENEMENT.

Men, Women and Children Perish Like Rats in a Trap in an Overcrowded Dwelling at the Corner of Fourteenth and Morris Avenues.

AN ENTIRE FAMILY WAS WIPED OUT.

Antonio Palmisano, His Wife and Two Children Victims of the Flames---Uggenio Casillo Loses Wife and Four Little Ones and Is Himself Injured--Cause of the Fire Unknown---Heartrending Scenes.

Headline from the *Newark Evening News* on March 12, 1900, reporting on the Italian immigrant tenement fire. Ultimately, fifteen individuals perished in the fire. *From the Newark Evening News, March 12, 1900.*

SILVER LAKE

The Italian enclave of the Silver Lake section of Newark continued to grow while Italian enclaves in other areas of the city began to shrink. Eventually, the Silver Lake section expanded into Belleville. Just like the other Italian enclaves in Newark, the Silver Lake neighborhood eventually warranted its own Roman Catholic church, the Church of the Immaculate Conception, incorporated in 1925.

The neighborhood's name came from the large artificial pond created in the nineteenth century by damming off a tributary of the Second River. At three hundred feet long and half a mile wide, it offered skating opportunities in the winter and boating in the summer. In 1866, the lake and property surrounding it was purchased by the Newark Ice Company to harvest ice in the winter for Newark.[70] On the evening of July 30, 1889, a storm caused the dam to burst, and it was not rebuilt. Despite the "lake" disappearing over a century ago, the name of the neighborhood remains.

"BECAUSE WE'RE ALL THE SAME"

This statement from Mari Ippolito is a testament to what I discovered during my interviews with descendants of the original Italian immigrants to Newark. Despite the neighborhood they may have lived in at the time or the church they attended, we're all the same.

Mari grew up in Silver Lake, and she provided an amazing account of her life with her extended family as well as her family history.

"I could walk to ten relatives' houses," Mari shared. "My mother's parents had a two-family house and we lived upstairs, and my grandma and grandpa lived on the first floor."

Surrounded by so many people in such a small area, Mari made sure to pay attention when the adults spoke so she could learn the family history.

"I listened when my grandmother talked," Mari told me. "I am the keeper of the family history."

Her great-grandmother Vincenza Severino was going to be sent to America to marry the husband of an aunt who had recently passed away. When Vincenza refused to go to America alone, her soon-to-be-husband, Angelo Longo, returned to Italy for their wedding. He stayed in Italy for six months and then returned to America to find a better job and home.

Mari's grandmother Teresina Longo was born in Cambasso, Calabria, in May 1897.

In 1902, Vincenza traveled to America with her now five-year-old daughter, Teresina. When she arrived at Ellis Island, Angelo wasn't there to meet her. He wasn't able to travel to New York. Thankfully, a priest saw Vincenza and her child and asked if she needed help. She explained she was waiting for her husband and didn't know what to do. The priest went to the Ellis Island officials and told them she was here to work in the church. As it turned out, the priest was from St. Anthony's, another Catholic church in Silver Lake. The priest was able to get her to her husband's home.

Teresina Longo, born in Cambasso, Calabria, in May 1897, came to America with her mother at age five. *Courtesy of Mari Ippolito.*

Vincenza and Angelo had five more children: Pasquale, Giuseppe, Nicholas, Anna Maria (Mary) and Luigi. Unfortunately, Mari's grandmother was not allowed to go to school. Instead, as the oldest sibling, it was her responsibility to take care of all the children.

"She was very smart, my grandma," Mari shared. "She taught herself to read and write in English and Italian. And she read the newspaper every Sunday."

As the boys grew up and needed to find work, they did what so many other Italians did—they Anglicized their names.

"The boys changed their names, so Luigi became Lou Long," Mari said. "Pasquale became Pat. Nicholas became Nick. Giuseppe became Joe. Because they could not get jobs; nobody would hire them."

The boys all completed their high school education and found work locally at Westinghouse, Charms Factory in Belleville and Wallace and Tiernan, a tool and die company.

"With just a high school education, they all did very well," Mari said.

Mari's grandmother Teresina married at sixteen. She had met her future husband, Gaetano "Tom" Riccio, while walking to Bloomfield

Center to pick up supplies to make pin bundles for the seamstresses. Mari's grandfather had immigrated from Greece at age fourteen, and his only possessions were three dollars and a stickpin. He came to America and never went back to Greece again. When Teresina asked if she could bring him home to meet her parents, her mother said no, that she would have an arranged marriage, just as she did. Thankfully, her father, Angelo, interceded and made sure she was able to marry for love.

Teresina married Gaetano in 1913, and they had their first child one year later. They had six children: Ferdinand "Fred," Francesco "Jake," Angelo, Vincenzo "Jidge" (his professional name became "Jack Carroll" as an actor and singer with Les Brown and His Band of Renown), Mary (Mari's mother, who was named for Teresina's sister) and Doretta "Dottie."

"I'm the youngest, and it was a way for me to connect," Mari shared. "I couldn't go forward, so I had to go back. I needed to feel a connection to my family."

Her family all continued to live in the area; even her uncle Jack Carroll did not move to California when his acting career took off. He made a movie and returned to New Jersey because he didn't want to be away from his family.

"I loved having all the family around. I mean, we had thirty-five people for Christmas Eve at my grandmother's in a four-room apartment," Mari told me.

One cherished item she owns is her grandmother's rolling pin. She uses it to make raviolis and cookies. Someday she will pass that beloved item on to her goddaughter. Her grandmother lived until she was ninety-one and Mari was twenty-four.

"I wouldn't trade it for the world. I think it was magnificent. I had absolute unconditional love from a tremendous amount of people," Mari shared.

I don't doubt that one bit.

"WE SPEAK AMERICAN"

Just as the men in Mari's family "Americanized" their names, there were many others who worked to leave their heritage behind in an effort to become "American," or what they thought was American.

Ken Burde's great-grandparents Palmo and Josephine immigrated from Bari, in the province of Puglia, with his grandfather Nicholas, his aunt Fiorentina "Florence" and uncle Lorenzo "Lawrence" when they were just children. When Palmo arrived at Ellis Island, he made his first move to be American. He changed the spelling of the family name from "Burdi" to "Burde" in order to look less ethnic.

Ken's great-grandfather opened a barbershop, and his clientele consisted of mostly Dutch businessmen. As his sons grew older, most became barbers as well. One son, Michael, drove a postal truck.

The father and his sons opened their own barbershop, Burde Brothers, and were known as "barbers and tonsorial artists." The family initially opened their shop in the First Ward, and after Ken's great-grandfather passed away, the barbershop moved to Silver Lake. Ken's uncle Lorenzo, nicknamed "Anzoo," also ran a billiard room in Silver Lake. When Ken's parents were married, they initially lived above the garage behind the building that housed the billiard room.

"When my parents were first married, they weren't sure where to go, so they lived above the garage on 215 Belmont Avenue," Ken shared. "They had a pot-belly stove for heat in the winter, and they called their place 'The Tree,' because it was up above the garage."

When Ken was a child and spent time at the barbershop, he gave shoeshines for a nickel.

"I remember being at the shop; he used to let me shine shoes," Ken said. "And I would get a nickel and then I'd go next door to the candy store and get some candy."

What was most important to his grandfather, however, was that he was considered "American."

"My grandfather had a heart attack, and the priest came over and prayed over him in Latin. Then he started speaking to my grandmother in Neapolitan," Ken said. "My grandfather sat up and said, 'We don't speak that language in here; get out!' The next day he got out of bed, went to Fewsmith Church and became a Presbyterian."

His grandfather Nicholas didn't allow anyone to speak either Italian or the regional Neapolitan language.

"We live in America; we speak American," Ken told me.

I don't think there was ever a doubt that Nicholas considered himself a proud American.

THE NEWARK ITALIAN COMMUNITIES

While the throngs of Italians that once made up a large part of the population of Newark have moved to other areas, they left an important footprint of their heritage throughout the city. They built the infrastructure of Newark, owned successful businesses and shared multiple places of worship that focused on their unique religious needs.

6

INFORMATION FOR THE COMMUNITY

NEWSPAPERS

First generation Italians are bound strongly to the foreign language paper.
Some few read newspapers printed in Italy, but the Italian-American papers
interest them more.
—*Charles W. Churchill,* The Italians of Newark

When southern Italian immigrants first arrived in the United States, their literacy rate was extremely low. This weakness was exploited at various times of America's history in an attempt to slow the tide of immigration from southern European countries. In 1912 and 1915, the U.S. Congress passed literacy requirements for incoming immigrants. Both bills were vetoed by Presidents William Howard Taft and Woodrow Wilson, respectively. The Immigration Act of 1917 required immigrants over sixteen to demonstrate basic reading comprehension in any language. The act was influenced by reports from commissions that believed a literacy test was the most practical way to reduce the number of immigrants arriving annually. The Immigration Act of 1917 remained in place until it was amended by the Immigration Act of 1924.

As Italian immigrants learned to read, they sought out newspapers, both in English and Italian, for information about their community and beyond. However, there was also a strong distrust of the media by Italian immigrants. Southern Italians had a suspicion of authority figures, including the Roman Catholic hierarchy and politicians. That distrust traveled with them when they immigrated to the United States. It is believed this distrust extended to the media in the United States due to the Italian press's role in social control.

It is hard to know how many papers were published, as even the official lists were not comprehensive (anarchist publications were not included), but according to an estimate, there were 150 Italian newspapers published in America between 1884 and 1944.[71] It is believed at one point in history there were as many as 15 weeklies being issued specifically for the Italian immigrant community; however, most of them were short-lived. Often a newspaper was launched to further the personal ambitions of its publisher or to vent his spleen against his adversaries. Most of the newspapers exerted little in the way of constructive influence on the immigrants.[72]

POPULAR NEWSPAPERS

Throughout the history of the Italian enclaves in Newark, several newspapers were popular based on an individual's preference and need. *La Rivista* was a short-lived weekly newspaper published from 1917 until 1921 by the Mattia Press, located on Crane Street.

Il Progresso Italo-Americano was unquestionably the leader among the first-generation immigrants.[73] The first daily Italian-language newspaper in the United States, *Il Progresso Italo-Americano* covered general news in Italy, as well as coverage of each Italian region. One page of each paper was devoted specifically to Italian news and activities in New Jersey. The paper was published daily for over a century, starting in 1880. In 1981, the paper was purchased by Italian investors for $1 million. The investors planned to expand coverage to include more news in English. At the time of the sale, the paper had a circulation of sixty thousand and was primarily focused on the greater New York metropolitan area.

In 1988, the National Labor Relations Board accused the publisher of negotiating in bad faith with two unions. Additionally, it was accused of moving its business in order to employ non-union workers. *Il Progresso Italo-Americano* was published in Emerson, New Jersey, where union employees producing the paper went on strike in late June and publication was halted in late July. At the same time, former employees of *Il Progresso Italo-Americano* began working on a new paper. *America Oggi* was developed as a similar Italian-language daily newspaper published in Norwood, New Jersey. In 2022, New York–based North Sixth Group purchased the global licensing rights to *America Oggi* and *Il Progresso Italo-Americano*. Both brands were integrated into America Domani, a digital media community for Italian Americans.

THE *ITALIAN TRIBUNE*

A long-standing source of information for Italian immigrants and Americans of Italian descent is the *Italian Tribune*. The weekly English-language newspaper has been in existence since 1931, with its offices originally located in Newark. In 2010, the paper's office moved from Newark to West Orange. The *Italian Tribune* was founded by Fred J. Matullo and John J. Sileo in 1931.[74]

"The publisher of the *Italian Tribune* aimed at creating an alternative to Italian language publications," current publisher Buddy Fortunato explained. "He realized the Italian immigrant was adjusting to an English-speaking country but wanted to maintain his ties to the Italian American community and his roots in Italy. The *Tribune* was the answer!"

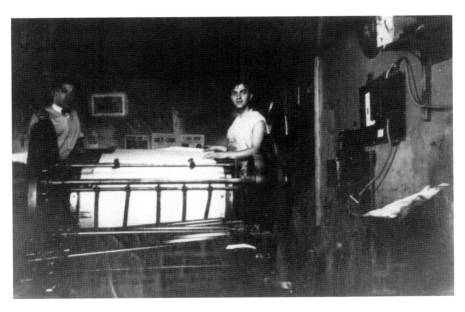

Frank and Freddie Matullo with a printing press at the office of the *Italian Tribune* on Garside Street. *Courtesy of Gerard Zanfini and Michael D. Immerso First Ward Italian collection; Charles F. Cummings New Jersey Information Center, Newark Public Library.*

In 1968, Ace Alagna, Fortunato's father-in-law, purchased the *Italian Tribune* and expanded its coverage and content beyond Newark's borders. The paper has seen multiple updates over the decades, including adding more long-form articles and features, similar to a magazine, to reach a wider audience, regardless of geographic location.

Fortunato assumed the duties of publisher on his father-in-law's retirement after serving as publisher for close to three decades. Since the change in duties, the paper's coverage has expanded again to the Northeast Corridor of Philadelphia, all of New Jersey and New York City and its boroughs.

"We have covered every positive story involving the Italian American community and became very involved in raising money for earthquakes in Italy, built nursery schools and purchased schoolbooks and supplies," Fortunato explained. "Our goal is to project the Italian and his contribution in America in every aspect of the American culture."

7

THE ROLE OF SOCIAL CLUBS AND MUTUAL AID SOCIETIES

When Italian immigrants arrived in the United States, there were very few sources for support. Many did not want to go to the government for a variety of reasons. Some were worried about deportation if they asked for assistance, while others brought a deep distrust of the government with them from their homeland. Social clubs and mutual aid societies helped fill that role.

Mutual Aid Societies

Mutual aid societies were a vital part of Italian immigrant communities in the United States, providing assistance navigating and adapting to their new community. These organizations provided basic needs, social and entertainment opportunities and a sense of extended community. These societies helped families start businesses, provided assistance when a family member was injured or killed on the job and helped with funeral expenses. They also offered healthcare, including basic medical care, prescription allowances and burial insurance. In short, mutual aid societies provided support for every part of an immigrant's life.

There were scores of mutual aid societies organized with limited membership. In Newark, for example, there were, among others, a Societa' Vallatese, a Societa' Caposelese and a Societa' Teorese. These associations

Members of Societa' Fraterno Amore (Caposelese Society) pose on Eighth Avenue at the intersection of Nesbit Street in 1924. *Courtesy of Gerard Zanfini and Michael D. Immerso First Ward Italian collection; Charles F. Cummings New Jersey Information Center, Newark Public Library.*

united the townsmen in mutual assistance and social activities.[75] They worked to carry on traditions of the confraternities of the Old Country and also sponsored feasts of the patron saints. While serving useful functions, these associations of townsmen also kept alive the sentiment of *campanilismo*.[76]

> *Campanilismo. This profoundly Italian expression refers to the love, pride and attachment to a certain place by those whose homes are located in the area metaphorically covered by the shadow of the local bell tower.*
> —*Parasecoli,* Al Dente

Certain Italian organizations also promoted Americanization. The Societa' San Gerardo Maiella fra Caposelesi, which was founded to handle Newark's festa, excluded from its membership all socialists, anarchists and atheists.[77]

> *Today only worn and tattered banners, lying in the chests of forgotten halls in various Italian quarters, recall these pioneer organizations.*
> —*Charles W. Churchill,* The Italians of Newark

While some mutual aid societies have persisted, many are long gone. According to Churchill's research in the early 1940s, the newer societies, such as the Sons of Italy, were better organized and financially sound. Many mutual aid societies were gradually transformed into social clubs and became centers of miniature regionalism within a general circle of regionalism.[78]

Social Clubs

Such organizations as these offer a great deal of pleasure to members in their sympathetic interest and their mutual dependence and constitute a refuge for those who have been disinherited by America.
—Charles W. Churchill, The Italians of Newark

While mutual aid societies focused on the financial, physical and spiritual, social clubs were primarily for social gatherings. My Uncle Sonny (Ettore Victor Fieramosca) was a member of the Tacoma Club and enjoyed playing cards with other men of the neighborhood. Clubs would sometimes have their own bocce courts and American baseball teams.

While social clubs were focused on recreation for Italian immigrants, there were times they came together to provide support for different events. When affairs of great interest to Italians arose, such as the Ital-Ethiopian War, members raised money and collected food and clothes for the homeland.[79] If a neighborhood individual or family was in need of support, different social clubs would become involved and provide support.

These organizations could be found in every Italian immigrant enclave around the country. The mutual aid

Lucille Ann Fieramosca and Ettore Victor "Sonny" Fieramosca, a member of the Tacoma Club. *Courtesy of Andrea Lyn Cammarato-Van Benschoten.*

Early photo of the membership of the Spilingesi Social Club in the Ironbound. *Courtesy of Cav. Prof. Eric Lavin.*

society became the safety net for the community, while the social club provided a break from the hard day-to-day lives and dangerous work these immigrants faced.

Over time, many mutual aid societies disbanded and so did many social clubs; however, a few clubs remain in Newark today. The Spilingese Social Club is still just a few steps away from Our Lady of Mount Carmel in the Ironbound on Oliver Street. The Spilingese Social Club was founded in 1927 in order to help newly arrived Italian immigrants and create a trusted point of contact for assistance. The club also helped any member of the community in need, whether they needed care for sick family or financial support for the unemployed. The club continues to be a source of pride and connection for those Italian Americans who call the Ironbound home.

The mutual aid society and social club were two important parts of the history and culture of Italian immigrant enclaves. They provided recreation and financial support. It was an example of paesani taking care of paesani.

8

THE IMPORTANCE OF FAMILY AND FOOD

When I first came here, Italian food wasn't anything I recognized. I didn't know what Italian American food was; we never ate it at home. It was the food of immigrants who came here and made use of the ingredients they had.
—Lidia Bastianich

While fast-food Italian has become a mainstream option for many, there are many more of us who grew up with Sunday dinner rituals that we consider authentic Italian cuisine.

In reality, it is more an Italian immigrant's twist on Sunday dinner that goes back generations. American "red sauce cuisine" is influenced by the traditions of Italian immigrants, but it is not Italian food. The cuisine is largely, although not exclusively, drawn from southern Italian recipes, though often these are not necessarily the domestic recipes Italian immigrants cooked in their homes. In this regard, red sauce cuisine is as much an invention of Americans as of Italians.[80] But as far as we were concerned growing up, this was a traditional Italian Sunday dinner, and no one could ever convince us of anything else.

The Sunday ritual in most homes often began with heading to church for mass, oftentimes arriving early to light candles and pray at the family's or neighborhood's patron saint. After mass, it was time to head to the cemetery to clean away the flowers from the previous week, scrub the headstones if needed and pray for the souls of the dearly departed. Then home. Grandma (or mom) would head to the kitchen to watch the gravy (and yes, in most of northern New Jersey, it's gravy). Meatballs were done either before going to church or after arriving home.

Once I was old enough to drive, my assignment, which I happily accepted, was to head to Di Paolo's Bakery on Bloomfield Avenue in the North Ward of Newark to pick up bread and pastries. Sometimes I would also pick up a cake. I was never told what to buy. I knew what everyone liked, and I went for a lot of the "regulars." Cannoli. Sfogliatella. Pignoli cookies. And of course a cup of coffee and a biscotti for me for the ride home.

The rest of the afternoon before dinner included going upstairs to my grandmother's to help set the table and getting chased away from the gravy pot as its thick red goodness continued to simmer until dinnertime. Dinnertime, by the way, was three o'clock—sharp. Dinner was macaroni, meatballs, sausage, braciole and a simple salad. After dinner was cake and coffee. And talking. Lots of talking. Sometimes loud and boisterous. Sometimes, but rarely, quiet. Lots of laughing. My cousins were my first friends. All of us sat at the card table (aka "the kid's table"), as oftentimes there just wasn't enough room at the "adult" table. Ironically enough, when the time came to move to the adult table, we lamented how we preferred being all together at the kid's table.

After dinner was when I learned how to play cards. The paper would get passed around the table. In the summer, we sat outside in the backyard and played board games until it was too dark to see. And laughed. Lots of laughing.

PEASANT FOOD

Growing up, some of the dishes that were easiest—and as it turns out, least expensive—to cook were family favorites. Some people referred to these dishes as "depression food" or "peasant food" for obvious reasons. Mothers and grandmothers learned tricks to stretch what was in the refrigerator so they could get every possible meal out of it. Have a little meat and gravy left from Sunday? Add some rice and make stuffed peppers. Have a leftover chicken? Make chicken broth and add some escarole and a can of cannellini beans with some crusty bread and you have a perfect hearty soup. These simple recipes are now considered high cuisine in many Italian restaurants today, and they get top dollar for them. Again, however, these recipes are often the evolution of recipes and meals immigrants brought with them and have become their own category under the Italian American food umbrella.

In most southern Italian towns, bread, vegetables such as lentils and fava beans and greens found in the wild were the staples. Pasta was considered a luxury. A peasant's lunch while working in the field could include a piece of bread, a small onion or a sardine.[81] Beans were often mixed with escarole or white chicory and made into a soup; more than likely this later became the Italian American favorite "escarole and beans." Immigrants would sometimes use chicken broth instead of plain water, another luxury they found in America.

When Italian immigrants arrived in America, the local grocer offered more options than they could have ever thought possible. Meat, which was a rarity in Italy, was now easily available. Pasta choices seemed almost endless. All these options turned Sunday dinner and holidays into a feast rarely enjoyed during their day-to-day lives in the Mezzogiorno.[82]

In the following pages, you'll find recipes for some of these simple, traditional and delicious dishes. Very few traditional recipes were documented. They often had statements like "a handful of this" or "soft, but not too soft," so often you use your best judgement and adjust to taste to your liking.

Escarole and Beans

If there was ever an ultimate "peasant dish," escarole and beans is it. It boils down to three main ingredients: escarole, cannellini beans and chicken broth. Oftentimes my grandmother would include some pepperoni in it as an extra treat, but it is just as delicious without it.

2 tablespoons olive oil
Chopped garlic
1 pound chopped escarole
4 cups chicken broth
1 (15-ounce) can cannellini beans, drained and rinsed
Salt and pepper
Grated Parmesan cheese
Pepperoni (optional)

Heat oil in large pot over medium heat. Add garlic.

Add escarole and cook until wilted; this will take only a few minutes. Add chicken broth, beans, salt and pepper.

Cover and cook over medium heat until beans soften; this should not take too long. Serve topped with grated cheese.

Giambotta

As the garden began to flourish, many Italian immigrants would use those vegetables to cook a taste of home that was both hearty and inexpensive. It was a staple for many Italian families from Naples south. Even though this is traditionally a dish associated with the gardens of summer, I always looked forward to it in the fall. It was a favorite dinner of mine growing up with a piece of crusty Italian bread saved from Sunday dinner. There are as many different versions of this recipe as there are spellings of its name, but this was the way it was made it my family.

2 tablespoons olive oil
Garlic
Potatoes cut into 4–6 pieces each
Crushed tomatoes
2 cups water
2 cups chicken broth
Onion (optional)
Squash
Zucchini
Basil
Italian parsley
Salt
Pepper

In a large pot, heat a little olive oil and garlic on low heat. Add potatoes and cook about 10 minutes until potatoes begin to soften.

Add tomatoes, water, chicken broth. Raise heat a little. Add onion (if using).

Add squash and zucchini. Add basil, Italian parsley, salt and pepper.

Continue to simmer and stir until a knife goes through the potatoes easily (but not too easily) and the squash is fork tender.

If you prefer a little thicker soup, add one tablespoon flour and mix thoroughly.

Pasta e Fagioli

It took me until I was a teenager to learn how to actually spell this delicious dish. Growing up, and even now, it is "pasta fazool."

Every Friday during Lent, dinner consisted of pasta e fagioli and a plain tomato pie. I'm not sure if everyone enjoyed it, but I know my Uncle Sonny and I certainly did. Growing up, we always had it "red," using some leftover Sunday gravy. It wasn't until I ordered it out at a restaurant once that I had it "white." I wasn't sure about it at first, but it definitely grew on me. Now, I actually ask for it white when I'm out from time to time.

No matter if you have it red or white, pronounce it "pasta e fagioli" or "pasta fazool," have it as dinner during Lent or an appetizer when you are out, it is always a great dish that hits the spot!

3 tablespoons extra virgin olive oil
2 garlic cloves, minced
2 (15-ounce) cans cannellini beans
16 ounces ditalini
1 teaspoon basil
4 cups Sunday gravy (or 1 28-ounce can of tomato sauce or crushed tomatoes)
½–1 cup chicken broth
Starchy water (from cooking the ditalini)
Salt
Black pepper

In a pot, warm the olive oil and garlic (don't let it burn). Add the beans to the garlic and oil and let simmer for 20 minutes, stirring periodically.

While the beans are simmering, cook the ditalini according to the directions until it is not quite done. When draining the ditalini, put a pot under the strainer to save the starchy water.

Pour the drained ditalini into the beans, olive oil, basil and garlic and mix together. Add the Sunday gravy or tomatoes and mix.

Add ½ cup chicken broth. Cook over medium heat until ditalini is completely cooked. Add salt and pepper to taste.

This is where personal taste comes in. Want the pasta e fagioli a little thicker? Add in one cup of starchy water at a time until it is the preferred consistency. Prefer a little more chicken broth? Add another ½ cup of broth. You prefer a little more garlic? Add it! Remember, you can always add. You can't remove.

Simple Italian Salad

After macaroni on Sunday, it was time for the salad. We never had salad before macaroni. And while it sounds like a fairly simple salad, there were always jokes about it. If Uncle Chubby was eating with us that day, don't put any cucumbers in the salad, because he wasn't able to eat them safely. If there were black olives in the salad, we would joke that it must have been a "special occasion." It was a simple salad, but it was just another point of discussion during dinner.

Iceberg lettuce
3–4 tomatoes on the vine
½ medium sweet onion
Oregano
Basil
Salt
Pepper
Oil
Red wine vinegar
1 cucumber, sliced (if Uncle Chubby wasn't there)
1 can black olives (if it was a special occasion)

Break up the lettuce into small pieces. Cut tomatoes into slices; usually about eight slices per tomato.

Peel and thinly cut the onion; mix with tomatoes.

Add oregano, basil, salt, pepper, oil and vinegar. Mix and place in refrigerator for at least 30 minutes to chill.

Stuffed Peppers

One of my absolute favorite dinners of all time is definitely stuffed peppers. Have a little extra chop meat from making meatballs on Sunday and some leftover gravy? Well, you're halfway there! Add some rice and grab a few bell peppers and there you go. This is another simple dish everyone will love. Unlike most recipes I grew up enjoying, this one was actually written down by my mother. I have the two pages written out longhand on yellow legal pad paper. I refer to them every time I make this recipe, just to be sure I'm not missing anything.

4–5 bell peppers
2 cups cooked rice
1 pound ground beef
Olive oil
Garlic powder
Diluted Sunday gravy

Use firm green bell peppers. Remove stems, cut opening into top of pepper and remove all seeds and membrane. Wash well and turn upside down to drain out all water.

Cook rice as per directions. After rice is finished, set aside and let cool until it is easily handled.

When rice has cooled, mix well with chop meat and stuff each pepper with rice/chop meat mix. Select a pot with a tight lid, large enough so the peppers can all stand up. Lightly coat the bottom of the pot with olive oil and garlic powder. Place peppers in pot; lightly sprinkle garlic powder over peppers. Add diluted Sunday gravy. When gravy begins to bubble, lower gas to a medium flame, cover and allow to cook slowly for about one hour.

Peppers are cooked when you press a knife blade against the side of the pepper and it offers *no* resistance.

Pastina

When they were sick, every Italian American child had pastina, often referred to as "Italian penicillin," made by their grandmother. No matter how old you may be when preparing this comfort food, you will remember days as a child when a grandmother's love could cure just about anything.

4 cups chicken broth
I cup pastina
I egg
Pecorino romano

Bring chicken broth to a boil. Add pastina and stir regularly; bring back to a boil. Remove from heat.

Lightly beat the egg and gently mix the egg into the pastina and chicken broth. Add pecorino romano.

You can add salt and pepper to taste if you would like, but I generally don't. The grated cheese provides the salty flavor many crave.

9
THE ROLE OF THE CHURCH

By 1900, there were 32,487 Italian-born immigrants living in the Archdiocese of Newark, and they had nine district Italian parishes. The census of 1880 showed only 1,547 Italian-born immigrants in the entire state.[83] When Italians began to arrive in the United States, the Irish establishment of the Catholic Church was unprepared for the difference in the style of worship Italian Catholics observed. And the Irish were not ready to accept the Italian form of Catholicism within the walls of Irish churches.

The Irish Catholics' approach to adoration was far more rigid than the Italian Catholics'. The Irish form of worship focused on the omnipotence of God with an emphasis on Jesus. This differed greatly from the belief in the divine and patron saints that makes up the rich part of the approach to Italian religion. Irish priests were horrified that the religious practices of Italian immigrants relegated God and Jesus to a secondary position.[84] The overwhelming opinion of the Irish clergy was the Italian immigrant approach to Catholicism was a blatant disrespect of God and the formal approach to church worship.

The Italians are a peculiar people and the habits and customs of their native land they would transplant in this country; but in time they will learn better.
—New York Freeman's Journal, *July 2, 1882*

Few Catholic churches existed in Newark during the late 1800s. The Catholic hierarchy of the New Jersey Diocese under Bishop Winnard Wigger began laying the foundation for the spiritual accommodation of the thousands of Catholic immigrants from all parts of Europe.[85]

BASEMENT CATHOLICS

While all that we have spoken of refers to the upper church, let it not be forgotten that we have three Masses in the basement for the Italians of the parish, and that Father Ferretti, under Father McLoughlin's direction does very efficient work for that portion of his flock.
—History of Transfiguration Parish-Mott Street, New York (1827–1897)

As a result of such negative opinions by the Irish Catholic clergy, Italian Americans became what the writer Alberto Giovannetti called "basement Catholics." In 1886, one immigrant remembered that "we Italians were allowed to worship only in the basement part of the Church at East 115th street in East Harlem."[86]

As Italian immigration to Newark continued to increase around the dawn of the twentieth century, the Archdiocese of Newark realized it had a serious problem. Italian immigrants were increasingly frustrated by their treatment by the Irish Catholic establishment. Some were establishing unauthorized parishes and private chapels within the confines of the Archdiocese of Newark. One unauthorized parish elected to leave the Catholic Church completely and organize under the Episcopal Diocese of Newark due to the requests ignored by the Catholic Archdiocese. Ultimately, the Irish Catholic establishment acquiesced and acknowledged parishes were needed to support the Italian immigrant community.

Initially, Italian Catholics in Newark assembled for worship in the old St. John's Hall on Mulberry Street, where the third bishop of Newark, Most Reverend Wigger, the son of German immigrants, established an Italian mission in 1882. They were originally ministered to by Reverend Albergo Vitola and later by Reverend Dr. Conrad Schotthoefer, a German who became fluent in Italian while preparing for the priesthood.

The newly arrived Italian immigrants were often incredibly poor, and there were not many priests who were able to speak the regional languages of the new immigrants.[87] As a result, the Italian immigrants were unable to financially support a local parish, as they frequently had the lowest-paying labor jobs, lived frugally and sent money home to family members still in Italy when they were able. By 1900, over thirty-two thousand Italians were living in the diocese with only nine total parishes. By American standards, they were considered "nominal Catholics."[88] The form of worship practiced by southern Italian immigrants differed greatly from that of the Catholic immigrants beyond the Irish pastoral establishment that arrived in the United States decades before the Italians. The longer established groups frequently did not understand or sympathize with the problems of the newcomers or look on their varying customs with favor.[89]

Bishop Wigger worked to fill this need and officially established the first parishes for Italians as a response to the continually growing population of Italian Catholics. The first three Italian parishes in Newark, under the charge of Father Schotthoefer, were St. Philip Neri's, Our Lady of Mount Carmel and St. Lucy's.

St. Philip Neri's Church

St. Philip Neri's Church was the first official Italian parish in Newark. Its cornerstone was laid in 1887 on Courthouse Square. It was opened to support the first Italian enclave of the city around Bank Street and Market Street in August 1888. Unlike the other Italian communities that would develop in all parts of the city, this Italian community was home to northern Italian immigrants.

In the following years, Italians from all over Newark attended services led by Father Schotthoefer.

The History of St. Philip Neri

Philip Neri was born in Florence in 1515. He was a Christian missionary and founder of the Congregation of the Oratory, a community of Catholic priests and laypeople. He spent his days ministering to anyone in need of assistance by talking to individuals anywhere they congregated in an effort to evangelize to those in Rome who had lost their way. During this time, election to the Sacred College in Rome was primarily a political process, and members were less than men of God. St. Philip Neri was beatified by Pope Paul V on May 11, 1615, and canonized by Pope Gregory XV on March 12, 1622. His feast day is May 26.

ST. PHIL NERI CHURCH AT COURTHOUSE SQUARE

I wished to stress the role of St. Philip for modern children.
It is very necessary.
—*Father Anthony Alomia, pastor of St. Philip Neri*

The Pallontine Fathers came to St. Philip Neri Parish in 1924. Father Alomia arrived in 1937. In an interview with Charles Wesley in 1942, he voiced concern over the deteriorating number of parishioners due to the construction of the new courthouse and the expanded commercialization of the area. The church had a total of 500 parishioners in 1942. During the first fifty-five years of the parish, the church had performed over 1,100 marriages and over 7,100 baptisms.[90]

St. Philip Neri Roman Catholic Church on Court House Place. *Courtesy of Gerard Zanfini and Michael D. Immerso First Ward Italian collection; Charles F. Cummings New Jersey Information Center, Newark Public Library.*

St. Philip Neri Church continued to serve Italians in the community for another twenty-six years and was permanently closed in 1968. The former location of the church is now a parking lot that is part of Essex County College. The church's sacramental records are now housed at Seton Hall University in South Orange, New Jersey.

Our Lady of Mount Carmel in Ironbound: "The Little Cathedral of Down Neck"

The Newark Archdiocese established a second Italian Catholic church in Newark in the Ironbound section of the city. In 1890, the Second Reformed Church on Ferry Street was purchased and became Our Lady of Mount Carmel Catholic Church. This was considered a "tacit admission of the native Protestant evacuation and the Italian occupation of the Down Neck area."[91] The Ferry Street Church's construction dates to 1848.

Our Lady of Mount Carmel

Our Lady of Mount Carmel is the title given to the Blessed Virgin Mary in her role as patroness of the Carmelite Order. The devotion to Our Lady of Mount Carmel originates at an Israeli worship location. In biblical times, it was where the prophet Elijah lived with hermits who prayed to God for salvation. The basis for honoring Mary under this title dates to her appearance to an English Carmelite in the thirteenth century. Mary gave him the Brown Scapular, a garment worn by the religious over the neck as a sign of her protection.

The wearing of the Brown Scapular by laypeople has come to mean accepting the Blessed Mother's love and trusting that Our Lady will protect them both in life and at the time of their death. Mary promised anyone who died while wearing the Scapular would not suffer in death and would be quickly released from purgatory. Our Lady of Mount Carmel's feast day is July 16. In addition to serving as the patroness of the Carmelite Order, she is the patron saint of protection from danger and for deliverance from Purgatory.

OUR LADY OF MOUNT CARMEL CHURCH

The Reverend Conrad Schotthoeffer was the first pastor of Our Lady of Mount Carmel. He then appointed Reverend Joseph Ali. Born in Turkey, Ali served with Father Schotthoefer at St. John's and was also previously curate at Saint Nicholas Church in Passaic and Saint Philip Neri in Newark. He remained as pastor until his death at the age of thirty-two in 1894.[92] Bishop Wigger then appointed Reverend Ernesto D'Aquila as pastor. Father D'Aquila was originally from Campobasso, Italy, a region adjoining the provinces many of the residents of Ironbound.[93] Under Father D'Aquila's guardianship, the Ferry Street Church was remodeled to better reflect the Italian culture of the parishioners.[94] He continued to serve as pastor to Our Lady of Mount Carmel for the next thirty-nine years. In 1932, in recognition of his care to his parish, His Holiness Pope Pius XI elevated Father D'Aquila to "Right Reverend Monsignor." A few months later, he was honored with the Knighthood of the Crown of Italy by King Victor Emmanuel III.[95] In 1933, Monsignor D'Aquila passed away. The office of pastor was temporarily filled by Reverend Gaetano Ruggiero before he moved on to St. Lucy's Church in the Old First Ward.

In 1933, Father Leonardo Viccaro was appointed pastor of Our Lady of Mount Carmel. Born in 1886, Father Viccaro was ordained in 1909. He arrived in the United States in 1922 and began his first assignment in the country at Holy Rosary Church in Jersey City, the first Italian parish in New Jersey. He then moved to Montclair as pastor and finally to Our Lady of Mount Carmel in the Ironbound.[96]

A parochial school was established under the direction of the Mission Sisters of the Sacred Heart, founded by Saint Frances Xavier Cabrini, who would later become the first American citizen to be canonized a saint.

MOTHER CABRINI

Maria Francesca Cabrini was born on July 15, 1850, in Sant'Angelo Lodigiano, in the Lombard Province of Lodi. She was the youngest of the thirteen children of farmers Agostino Cabrini and Stella Oldin. Born prematurely, she was in frail health her entire life. At age thirteen, Francesca attended a school run by the Daughters of the Sacred Heart of Jesus and graduated cum laude with a teaching certificate.

The altar inside Our Lady of Mount Carmel in the Ironbound at Christmastime. *Courtesy of Andrea Lyn Cammarato-Van Benschoten.*

After her parents passed away, she applied to the Daughters of the Sacred Heart. However, she was rejected due to her poor health. Instead, she became the headmistress of the House of Providence orphanage in Codogno. Over time, she developed a small group of women who wanted to live a pious way of life. In 1877, Francesca took religious vows and added Xavier to her name to honor the Jesuit saint Frances Xavier, the patron saint of missionary service. In 1880, she founded the Missionary Sisters of the Sacred Heart of Jesus and remained its superior general until her death in 1917.

In September 1887, Francesca sought the approval of Pope Leo XIII to establish missions in China. Instead, he urged her to go to the United States to help the Italian immigrants who were

Portrait of Mother Francis Xavier Cabrini, 1880. She was the first American citizen to be canonized a saint. *Courtesy of Gerard Zanfini and Michael D. Immerso First Ward Italian collection; Charles F. Cummings New Jersey Information Center, Newark Public Library.*

emigrating at a rapid rate. These immigrants were almost all poverty-stricken and in need of support. She and six other sisters of her order arrived in New York City in March 1889.

Monsignor Ernest D'Aquila contacted Francesca and asked her to come to Our Lady of Mount Carmel to help educate the children of the newly arrived Italian immigrants. She agreed, and in 1899, she started a parochial school in the basement of Our Lady of Mount Carmel. Later she moved the school to two adjoining storefronts the children called "The House of Glass."[97]

Everything was lacking, there were no comforts of any kind, but there were Italian sisters who spoke their language. The children sensed that they were loved by them and were happy and faithful to their poor classrooms.
—*Mother Frances Xavier Cabrini*

Top: Monument honoring Mother Francis Xavier Cabrini. The monument is located in a small park in the Ironbound, where the school she created once stood. *Courtesy of Andrea Lyn Cammarato-Van Benschoten.*

Home support for the children of Italian immigrants was also a great need. Some parents were financially unable to care for their children, while other children were orphaned once they arrived in the United States, left to the care of the community or the state. In 1903, a local newspaper reported that "the building known to all old residents of the West Hudson towns…as the 'Ludlow Mansion,' has been transformed into a home for orphan girls of Newark and vicinity." The orphanage was named in honor of St. Anthony[98] and was able to initially house seventy-eight girls.

There is a statue of Mother Cabrini at Cabrini Park, outside of Penn Station in Newark, which is the site of the old Mount Carmel Church where she founded her school for the immigrant children.

THE "NEW" OUR LADY OF MOUNT CARMEL

In 1943, Reverend Richard Calligaro was appointed as administrator and spiritual leader of the parish. Realizing the membership was in need of a new church, recreational center and rectory, he went before the Most Reverend Archbishop Walsh with his request. Archbishop Walsh granted Father Calligaro permission to purchase five additional lots adjacent to the school. However, the project would not officially move forward until 1953, when His Excellency, the Most Reverend Thomas Boland, became spiritual head of the See of Newark after the death of Archbishop Walsh. The groundbreaking of the church took place during the summer of 1953.[99]

The parish membership set out to raise the necessary funds for their new spiritual home. In ten weeks, they had already raised $260,000 of the

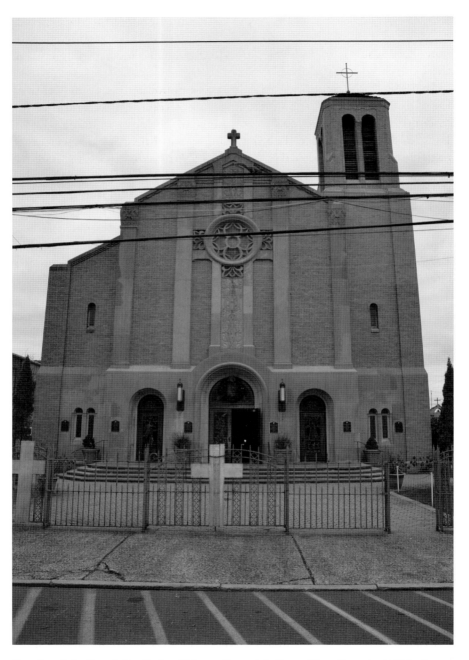

Exterior of the "new" Our Lady of Mount Carmel, built on Oliver Street in 1955 in the Ironbound. Our Lady of Mount Carmel is the third-oldest Italian Catholic parish in New Jersey. *Courtesy of Andrea Lyn Cammarato-Van Benschoten.*

$350,000 needed for the project, and within fifteen months, 70 percent of the money promised had been paid. Father Calligaro personally donated the statue of Our Lady of Mount Carmel for the Sanctuary of the Church.[100]

In 1949, Father Francis Di Giorgio was appointed as a new priest to Our Lady of Mount Carmel. He and Father Calligaro worked together to continue to build the parish and move all masses to the "new" Our Lady of Mount Carmel. The new Church on Oliver Street welcomed parishioners in August 1955. In 1968, there were two Our Lady of Mount Carmel Churches: the "old" church on Ferry Street continued to hold mass while the "new" church on Oliver Street began holding mass. Father Calligaro retired, and in 1972, Father Di Giorgio was named pastor. In 1975, the decision was made to suspend masses at the "old church" on Ferry Street, and the property was to be sold. Shockingly, in 1979, Father Di Giorgio died suddenly and unexpectedly. Two months later, Reverend Di Pasquale was appointed pastor.

A Grandmother's Gift of Faith

She really integrated me into the life of that parish. I would say the greatest gift she ever gave me was the gift of the faith, which I still hold near and dear in my heart today.
—Cavaliere Professore Eric Lavin

Many I have chatted with agree it was our grandmothers who had the biggest impact on our lives. And for Cav. Prof. Eric Lavin, his earliest memories of attending mass at Our Lady of Mount Carmel are no different. His grandmother Antonia Calello emigrated from Spilinga in the Italian region of Calabria in 1955, right at the start of the Our Lady of Mount Carmel's new church on Oliver Street.

"My fondest memories were every day my grandmother, who was my best babysitter, would holler at me Italian to get going and we'd mosey on down and go to daily mass," Eric shared. "She really integrated me into the life of that parish. I would say the greatest gift she ever gave me was the gift of the faith, which I still hold near and dear in my heart today."

Eric's grandmother was in attendance when the new church on Oliver Street was solemnly opened on August 21, 1955. Eric's American family story was built in concert with the story of Our Lady of Mount Carmel.

He knows the history of the parish by heart. It is obviously his "passion," as he puts it, to help keep the 134-plus-year-old parish flourishing.

"But my role, my function, my dream, my desire, my passion, my love, is to keep this church going. It's withstood the test of time. It's withstood a lot of history in Newark," Eric said. "But my goal is just to keep that story going."

Eric, I have no doubt your passion for your faith and your love for Our Lady of Mount Carmel will keep that parish going long into the future.

Antonia Calello, grandmother of Eric Lavin, immigrated to the Italian community in the Ironbound in 1955. She provided Eric with "the greatest gift of faith." *Courtesy of Cav. Prof. Eric Lavin.*

ST. LUCY'S CHURCH

We all need a place to celebrate our treasure, our customs and our devotion, a place where we can go where everything is the same as it was for our ancestors. That sacred place and space is St. Lucy's. St. Lucy's is our spiritual home, just as it was the spiritual home of our parents, grandparents, and great-grandparents since 1891.
—Reverend Thomas D. Nicastro, VF, The Feast of St. Gerard Mailla C.Ss.R

As the Italian population of the First Ward continued to grow into what would become the fifth-largest Italian immigrant community in the country, so did the need for their own Catholic parish. St. Lucy's Roman Catholic Church was organized as a mission church of St. Philip Neri, and its original wood-frame church was incorporated in 1891 on Sheffield Street. Its cornerstone was laid on December 13, the feast day of Saint Lucy. Like the congregations in many other Italian enclaves, St. Lucy's Church became the heart and soul of the Old First Ward. It ultimately grew to become a national parish with forty thousand Italians in its jurisdiction.[101]

SANTA LUCIA

The church's namesake, Santa Lucia, was martyred in Syracuse (Sicily) in the third century. She is the patron saint of the blind as well as those afflicted with eye diseases.

In 303, the Roman emperor Diocletian issued an edict outlawing Christianity in the Roman Empire. Christian churches and sacred texts, such as scripture and liturgical books, were to be destroyed. However, Lucia continued to worship in secret and began to give away her dowry to the poor.

The original St. Lucy's Church on Sheffield Street, built in 1892. *Courtesy of Gerard Zanfini and Michael D. Immerso First Ward Italian collection; Charles F. Cummings New Jersey Information Center, Newark Public Library.*

When the suitor her parents had arranged for her to marry learned she had been giving away her worldly possessions to aid the poor, coupled with study of the Christian faith, he reported her to the governor of Syracuse, denouncing her as a Christian. Ultimately, she was martyred for her faith in God.

Saint Lucy is often depicted holding her eyes because legends state either the guards gouged her eyes out as torture or that she gouged her own eyes out so her suitor would no longer be tempted by their beauty.

SAINT LUCY'S IN THE FIRST WARD

The brick-and-stone church structure that has welcomed generations of worshippers was not built until 1925–26. Like the original wood-frame church, the new church was dedicated on St. Lucy's Feast Day, December 13. The architect was Neil Convery, and ecclesiastical artist Gonippo Raggi painted the church's murals. Raggi also worked on the Cathedral-Basilica of the Sacred Heart in Newark.

In 1897, Bishop Wigger appointed Reverend Joseph M. Perotti pastor of St. Lucy's, and the parish was canonically erected, officially separating it from St. Philip Neri Church. Father Perotti, born in northern Italy, arrived at St. Lucy's after serving for a short period in New York and Boston.[102]

Father Perotti had many concerns when he arrived at the newly formed parish. He was greatly concerned about the extreme poverty of his parishioners. He was concerned for the financial stability of St. Lucy's, which was already deeply in debt. A fire in the church in 1902 added to the challenges he faced as he attempted to provide stability for his parishioners. His greatest worry, however, was the education and welfare of the children of the Old First Ward.

Just as Monsignor D'Aquila asked Frances Cabrini to aid in educating the youth of Our Lady of Mount Carmel, Father Perotti made the same request. Mother Cabrini's missionaries came to St. Lucy's in 1902. However, even this future saint could not overcome the poverty of the parish, and after one year the school was abandoned.[103] Later the school project was continued by the Sisters of St. John the Baptist in 1906.

The parish continued to grow. More than 10,000 baptisms were performed between 1910 and 1920, with 1,100 recorded in a single year.[104] However, Father Perotti faced a serious financial issue. The numerous feasts held out of the church were not under the control of St. Lucy's but

Mural on the ceiling of St. Lucy's Church. The murals inside the church were painted by ecclesiastical artist Gonippo Raggi. *Courtesy of Andrea Lyn Cammarato-Van Benschoten.*

under the various societies that organized them. As a result, the church received very little of the funds raised by each feast. The church was in a tenuous financial position, yet he did all he could to continue with the plan of a new church.

Later Father Perotti was elevated to the status of domestic prelate with the title of monsignor. He received his title from Bishop Walsh several years before his death and was a widely loved and respected member of the First Ward community. Monsignor Perotti continued as pastor until his death in the fall of 1933. At the time of his passing, his death was mourned by thousands, especially the members of the St. Lucy's Parish. When Bishop Walsh shared his eulogy with the mourners, he invited anyone who doubted Monsignor Perotti's devotion to the church and his flock to visit his bare room. He gave all he had to the poor of the church. He had no possessions—only fifty cents and the clothes on his back. He was buried at Holy Sepulchre Cemetery in East Orange, New Jersey, in a grave donated by two parishioners.[105]

Several months after the death of Monsignor Perotti, the bishop appointed Father Ruggiero pastor in 1934, a position he held until his death on February 14, 1966. Father Gaetano (Cajetan) Ruggiero immigrated to Newark in 1921 and was Monsignor Perotti's assistant from 1922 to 1931. One of his first decisions as pastor was to insist all feasts be conducted under the auspices of St. Lucy's. There were multiple strong objections to the plan, but ultimately, the societies relented. As a result of this new financial support to the church, Father Ruggiero was able to complete the interior of the new St. Lucy's in six months. The decision to move the feasts under the church financially saved the church and ensured its future. He served as the church's pastor for thirty-two years until his death in 1966. His wish was to be buried on the grounds of St. Lucy's, on the side of the church near the grotto of Our Lady of Lourdes in the St. Gerard Garden, forever linked to his beloved St. Lucy and St. Gerard.[106]

In 1955, Father Joseph Granato arrived at St. Lucy's. In his first year at the parish, he worked with the Drum and Bugle Corp., the Catholic Youth Organization (CYO) and the Sodality. A few short months later, Father Joseph Nativo, known lovingly to parishioners as "Father Nat," was assigned to St. Lucy's as well. Father Nat then took over the responsibilities of the Drum and Bugle Corp., the CYO and the Sodality from Father Granato. Additionally, Father Nativo formed the St. Lucy's Men's Choir in 1956, and it remained under his direction for its first decade in existence. Jerry DeGrazio then led the choir for the next twenty-five years.[107]

Reverend Donzillo, Monsignor Perotti and Reverend Ruggiero, circa 1920. *Courtesy of Gerard Zanfini and Michael D. Immerso First Ward Italian collection; Charles F. Cummings New Jersey Information Center, Newark Public Library.*

Father Granato's and Father Nativo's tenures at St. Lucy's proved a huge challenge as the concept of "urban renewal" hit the Old First Ward full force, destroying almost all of the original Italian immigrant neighborhood. By the end of the redevelopment of the neighborhood, just about all that remained was St. Lucy's, a few street names and a small number of original businesses. Between 1966 and 1971, St. Lucy's had multiple temporary administrators who did not understand the culture and community of the church and those who continued to return for worship, despite the destruction of their beloved neighborhood.

> *When Father Ruggiero died, we thought we were finished then, and that was in 1966. And then unfortunately, we had five years of temporary administrators who really didn't understand what this was all about.... Father Nativo and I were hamstrung, we couldn't say anything, and we couldn't do anything. But in 1971, I was appointed temporary administrator. And I wrote once in our centennial memorial, an unwritten pact was made between us and the people; if you stay, we'll stay. And we both did. We all did. So we survived Father Ruggiero's death. We survived the Newark Riots. We survived Columbus Homes.[108]*
> —*Monsignor Granato*

Father Nativo served the flock of St. Lucy's for almost fifty years, until his passing in July 2004. His Vigil Mass was officiated by his longtime friend Monsignor Granato. The third pastor, Monsignor Joseph Granato, served the parish faithfully for fifty-four years, until June 2009. Monsignor Granato passed away on December 9, 2021.

The following of St. Gerard became so popular, in 1977, the National Conference of U.S. Bishops made St. Lucy's the National Shrine of St. Gerard. Additionally, in 1998, St. Lucy's Church was added to the New Jersey State and National Registers of Historic Places. The Sanctuary of St. Gerard was designed by Luigi Vivoli of Grantwood, New Jersey.

> *All the doors lead into the nave of the church. Upon entering the nave, the sweep of high arches carried by the marble columns on both sides leads the eye to the sanctuary and to the elaborate apse with its high altar.*
> —*National Register of Historic Places Registration Application for St. Lucy's Church*

They Brought Their Saints with Them

As immigrants continued to arrive in the First Ward and found their way to pray at St. Lucy's, they were compelled to bring their devotion to the patron saints, specifically the patron saint of their town (*paese*). The priests, being Italian themselves, understood the cultural significance of patron saints in their daily prayer. They also understood their external demonstration of expressing their customs and rituals connected with the celebration of a saint's feast day.[109] Throughout the church, statues of each patron saint were carefully placed for prayers from their devotees.

Statues of the different villages include:

Maria Incoronata (Sant' Andrea di Conza)
Santa Maria della Neve (Calabritto)
St. Michael (Maddaloni)
St. Rocco (Lioni)
St. Sebastiano (Marigliano)
Our Lady of Mt. Carmel (Avigliano)
Maria dell' Assunta di Piemo (San Fele)
St. Sabino (Atripalda)
Maria Incoronata (Recigliano)
St. Nicolo (Teora)
St. Vito (Castelgrande)
St. Gerard Maiella (Caposele)

In addition to the statues that are venerated throughout the church, there are several stained-glass windows in honor of the different patron saints from immigrant villages, including St. Mark (Manocalzati).

St. Rocco's Church of the Fourteenth Ward

Italians continued to immigrate to all areas of Newark. As a result, their need for places of worship that understood their unique approach to Catholicism continued to expand.

St. Rocco's Church, originally part of the Fourteenth Ward, now known as the Central Ward, was established in 1899 as an Italian mission. Its first place of worship was in a small church on Bedford Street. It took more than

Statue of Santa Maria della Neve (Our Lady of the Snows) brought by Italian immigrants from the commune of Calabritto. *Courtesy of Andrea Lyn Cammarato-Van Benschoten.*

Exterior of St. Rocco's Church of the Old 14th Ward, now referred to as the Central Ward. The church was formed in 1899 as an Italian mission; however, its permanent structure was not completed until 1937. *Courtesy of Andrea Lyn Cammarato-Van Benschoten.*

ten years for the current structure to be completed. It became an official parish under Father Umberto Donati in 1918, who served as pastor of St. Rocco's until 1941. The incorporation of St. Rocco's Parish meant that the Fourteenth Ward colony of Italians had become "large and important enough" to have its own church.[110]

ST. ROCCO

St. Rocco was a fourteenth-century man born in Montpellier, France, to a family of nobility. Both of his parents had died by the time he turned twenty. At that point, he gave away all his worldly goods, refused the title of governor and made a pilgrimage to Rome.

121

At the time, bubonic plague was devasting the provinces of Italy. He continually offered his assistance at hospitals, caring for the sickest of all patients. Many of those in his care were healed and survived, and they credited St. Rocco's care and intercession on their behalf. He traveled from town to town caring for the ill and performing miracles by healing many of the sickest he encountered.

After years of healing many in Italy, including himself, when he was beset with the plague, he returned to Montpellier. Sadly, he was believed to be a spy and jailed; the judge who sentenced him was his paternal uncle and unaware he was sentencing his nephew. Rocco died in prison at the age of thirty-two.

St. Rocco is venerated as the protector against the plague and all contagious diseases. Nowhere else in the world honors St. Rocco as significantly as southern Italy and Sicily. Not long after his death, southern Italy suffered multiple cholera epidemics, and the people turned to St. Rocco for his protection.

ST. ROCCO'S CHURCH

Despite its incorporation at the turn of the century, it took quite a bit of time to build the actual structure. Father Donati continually worked to raise the necessary funds to build the church. Members of the congregation who were out of work at the time voluntarily supplied their labor in lieu of financially supporting the endeavor.[111] The basement of the church, a familiar spot for Italian Catholics in Newark, opened in March 1927. Challenges raising funds during the difficult years of the Depression persisted. However, Father Donati was undeterred and continued to raise funds for the completion of the church. Ten years later, on May 9, 1937, the upper church structure was officially dedicated.

The Italian/Mediterranean structure was created by architect Neil J. Convery, who also designed St. Lucy's in the First Ward and Sacred Heart in the Vailsburg section of Newark. Its design was based on St. Balsius' Church in Lendinara, within the Province of Rovigo, in Italy. This was the church Father Donati admired as a student forty years earlier.[112] Its design is in the Italo-Byzantine style with a basilica-type dome, making it one of the few domed churches in the city. The paintings on the ceiling of the church were painted by Luigi Aulicino. St. Rocco's is not a neo-Italian modern but clearly period architecture in the true Italian spirit of quaint, picturesque design.[113]

Statues of St. Nicola (*left*), St. Rocco (*center*) and St. Cataldo (*right*) on the exterior of St. Rocco's Church on Hunterdon Street. *Courtesy of Andrea Lyn-Cammarato Van Benschoten.*

In 1941, Reverend Joseph De Sanctis took over as pastor of St. Rocco's Church. During his tenure, statues were added to the front niches, and the basement was adapted to serve as a recreation, education and community space. In 1955, St. Rocco School opened.

In 1980, St. Rocco's Church was added to the State and National Registers of Historic Places. In 2005, it was announced by the Archdiocese of Newark that St. Rocco and St. Ann Parishes would merge, and St. Rocco would no longer be used as a place for Catholic worship. It does, however, remain on the State and National Registers of Historic Places and is currently home to the New Calvary Church.

CHURCH OF THE IMMACULATE CONCEPTION

Originally created as an Italian Mission of St. Anthony's Church in the Silver Lake section in 1922, the Church of the Immaculate Conception was incorporated in 1925 by Bishop O'Connor. Reverend Cataldo Alessi led the parish for its first three years of mission status. Immaculate Conception had humble beginnings with a small congregation of seventy-five, and

Mass was celebrated in an old movie theater on Mt. Prospect Avenue. Reverend Francis P. Mestice was named pastor in 1925, and a certificate of corporation was filed to rate the mission as a National Apostolate in the same year. Father Mestice was born in 1886 in Potenza and was ordained in 1910. He immigrated to the United States in 1920. He remained pastor of Immaculate Conception for thirty-three years. Upon incorporation, the church took the name of Immaculate Conception Church and moved to its new location on Summer Avenue, which included a hall where children could receive religious instruction. Members of the parish often referred to their new place of worship as the "little Italian Church."

As the church grew, so did their groups and organizations. The Holy Name Society, the Rosary Society and the Addolorata Society were all formed under the auspices of Immaculate Conception.

THE IMMACULATE CONCEPTION

In the sixth month, the angel Gabriel was sent from God to a town of Galilee called Nazareth, to a virgin betrothed to a man named Joseph, of the house of David, and the virgin's name was Mary. And coming to her, he said, "Hail, favored one! The Lord is with you." But she was greatly troubled at what was said and pondered what sort of greeting this might be. Then the angel said to her, "Do not be afraid, Mary, for you have found favor with God. Behold, you will conceive in your womb and bear a son, and you shall name him Jesus. He will be great and will be called Son of the Most High, and the Lord God will give him the throne of David his father and he will rule over the house of Jacob forever, and of his kingdom there will be no end."
—Luke 1:26–33

The Blessed Virgin Mary's Immaculate Conception was defined and proclaimed to be dogma in 1854. Prior to the 1854 definition, many theologians pointed to Luke 1:28: "Hail, full of grace." This verse was meant to say Mary was always filled with grace and, as a result, without sin.

The Feast of the Immaculate Conception is one of the most important holidays on the Catholic calendar. It became an official holiday in 1854, as declared by Pope Pius IX. In traditional Italian beliefs and forms of adoration, images and icons are not simply an aid to prayer. It is believed they provide a source of power, protection and blessings. That level of devotion came with those who immigrated to the United States, and for many, that devotion has continued through the generations.

The "Little Italian Church" of Newark

Just as Immaculate Conception Church began its official life, the Great Depression took hold of the entire country. The financial challenges of the community hit the church hard, and it was often in fear of closing. Still, it continued to persevere for decades.

In 1958, Reverend Joseph Cestaro became the new pastor, and the church started to turn toward financial stability. After years of fundraising, the Holy Name Society raised enough funds for a new site on Woodside Avenue. In September 1964, a groundbreaking ceremony took place, and the new church was dedicated just shy of two years later in 1966. Archbishop Thomas B. Boland officiated the dedication of the new Immaculate Conception Church.

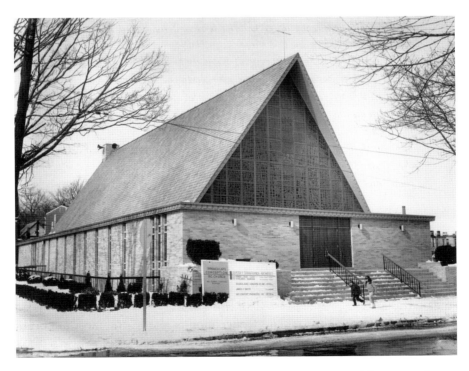

The façade of Immaculate Conception Church on Summer Avenue served the community known to many as North Newark. *Courtesy of the Roman Catholic Archdiocese of Newark.*

In 1969, Reverend Benjamin Piazza was sent to Immaculate Conception Church as the new administrator. He was officially named its pastor in 1974. On the fiftieth anniversary of the church, Father Piazza was named dean of the parishes of North Newark.

The three original societies of the church expanded to offer additional programs to parishioners, including scouting, a daycare, a senior citizen group and a choir, to name a few.

By 1975, over two hundred neighborhood children attended CCD (Confraternity of Christian Doctrine) religious education classes at the church and the church was home to three thousand parishioners.

In 2000, Immaculate Conception Church celebrated its seventy-fifth anniversary. In 2005, the parish of Immaculate Conception Church was combined with the parish of Our Lady of Good Council.

FEASTS

The Italians are not a sensitive people like our own. When they are told that they are about the worst Catholics that ever came to this country, they don't resent it or deny it. If they were a little more sensitive to such remarks they would improve faster. The Italians are callous as regards religion.
—*Lydio F. Tomasi, "American Views of Italian Newcomers"*

A popular form of celebration by Italians in Roman Catholic religious life has long been feasts for their patron saints. In Italy, during the annual celebrations of a town's patron saint, it was customary to take the statue of the saint from the church and carry it, in procession, through the streets.[114] Just as Italian immigrants brought many of their religious beliefs with them, so came the idea of the patron saint feast and procession.

The Irish Catholic hierarchy of the American Catholic Church were particularly offended by this display of faith. They often did not consider these feasts religious events and felt they were steeped in pagan ritual, full of religious apathy. Irish clergy, and their followers, commented bitterly on the "heathen" quality of Mezzogiorno worship.[115]

Italian immigrant feasts were also not without controversy. Saint Rocco's feast in 1891 was marred by tragedy when a copper casing filled with fireworks exploded outside Alfonso Ilaria's saloon on Boyden Street.[116] While many of the original feasts that were celebrated by Italian immigrants no longer take place, there are still a few in Newark that draw generations of Americans of Italian descent back to the "old neighborhood."

The Feast of Saint Gerard

To the uninitiated, the spectacle can be at once inspiringly devout and shockingly crass, as participants push their way through the throngs to pin ribbons, capes and even blankets made of money in various denominations to the somber cloth habit draping a life-size statue of the saint.
—*Mary Ann Castronovo Fusco, "CITY LIFE; How a Church Brings Life to Newark's Little Italy,"* New York Times, *October 10, 1999*

Of all the feasts that took place in the Old First Ward of Newark, the Feast of St. Gerard was the most significant and continues 125 year later. The earliest manifestation of devotion to Saint Gerard in the First Ward is attributed to the Caposelesi immigrants who brought this devotion with them from the shrine at Materdomini.[117] It was the Caposelese Society under which

The Very Reverend Cavaliere Thomas D. Nicastro, VF, preparing for the procession during the Feast of St. Gerard. *Courtesy of the Very Reverend Cav. Thomas D. Nicastro, VF.*

the feast was originally organized. Since then, the feast has been an annual tradition around his feast day on October 16.

SAINT GERARD MAIELLA

Born in 1726 in the Italian town of Muro, Gerard was the youngest of four surviving children born to Dominic and Benedetta Maiella. Born in frail health, he was rushed to the local church to be baptized, should his life be cut short. While he did live to adulthood, his health was always frail, and he died on October 16, 1755, at the age of twenty-nine.

Despite his poor health, he went to work as a tailor's apprentice when his father died while he was quite young. His earnings were split between his family, caring for the poor and giving to the church for the souls in purgatory. Benedetta, his mother, knew he was meant for a holy life beyond that of a tailor, as he was loving and prayerful.

Young Gerard attempted to join two religious orders but was rejected by both due to his ill health. He was finally accepted by the Congregation of the Most Holy Redeemer.

In 1753, a woman wrote a letter and accused him of having an affair with a local woman. He offered no defense. As a result, he was found guilty of the charge and was denied receiving Holy Communion. Brother Gerard's only comment was, "There is a God in Heaven, and He will prevail."

Months later, as the accuser lay on her death bed, she admitted to making up the story. When the lie was learned, Brother Gerard was released from his denial of Holy Communion. He did not seek announced vindication. He felt the will of God had been fulfilled. And that was enough for him.

In 1755, Brother Gerard was bedridden with hemorrhages and dysentery. As the end of his life grew near, he had a sign placed on the door of his room that noted, "Here the will of God is done, as God wills, and as long as God wills." He died at twenty-nine of tuberculosis on October 16, 1755, in Materdomini, Italy.

The Story of the Miraculous Handkerchief

After visiting the home of friends, Brother Gerard forgot his handkerchief. One of the young daughters of the family ran to him, calling, "Brother Gerard, you forgot your handkerchief." He responded, "Keep it; it will be useful to you some day." That handkerchief became a precious family heirloom. Many years later, when that daughter was in danger of dying while delivering her child, she remembered the words of Brother Gerard and asked for the handkerchief and placed it on her womb. Both she and her child were saved from death.

After that miraculous recovery, the handkerchief was passed from woman to woman expectant with child in the prayerful hope it would help them deliver a healthy baby. Some families took threads from the handkerchief to keep with them. At the time he was canonized on December 11, 1904, only a small piece remained. It was enough, however, to pass its graces on to other fabric touched to it.

Now new handkerchiefs with St. Gerard's likeness, also touched to his relics, are given to visitors to the International Shrine of St. Gerard Maiella in Materdomini, Italy, as well as at the national shrine in Newark. He is now widely accepted as the patron saint of expectant mothers, children, the unborn and, of course, generations of the original immigrants of the Old First Ward of Newark.

The St. Gerard Feast at St. Lucy's Church: A Living Memory

"Did you catch something that you just said that only people who really lived that part of the feast would refer to it the way you did? Really, what you just say?"

That was the question posed to me during my chat with the Very Reverend Cav. Thomas D. Nicastro, VF. It took me a minute to think what grabbed Father's attention.

"He."

As we discussed the throngs of people that attended the Feast of St. Gerard every year, we talked about how the family would converse around the dinner table on the Sunday of the feast and try to decide when to head to the church, thinking about when "he" would move away from the church and start the procession.

"Where 'he' is. You made it sound like you were talking about a real person and not a statue. Everybody that grew up there would say, 'Where is he?'" Father Nicastro said. "Everybody who grew up there had a relationship with him, like he was your friend, and you referred to 'him' and not to a statue."

It was an interesting distinction Father Nicastro pointed out to me, one that I never really considered before, but he was 100 percent correct. We all had—and have—a special friendship with St. Gerard. He has always been our protector and guide. We feel both a sense of love for him, as well as protection of him, as we feel like he is a member of our collective Old First Ward community.

Father Nicastro's family settled in the Old First Ward at the turn of the century. His maternal grandparents, Domenico and Anna (Maria Nicola) Miano, were married in the original wood-frame St. Lucy's Church in October 1914. The devotion his family had for St. Gerard was instilled in him from a young age. He calls it "a living memory."

"Get-togethers with nanna and nonno, with your grandmother's and your grandfather's passion and love for food and everything about it. Friendship over meals, gardens, fig trees along with homemade wine. This great treasure of theirs has become our heritage and lasting legacy to each of us in the vital role that they play in American history, culture and folklore of North America," Father Nicastro said. "It is our responsibility to pass on this heritage. This pride of life and everything that we do. They've given to us a living memory, a memory that's not stagnant but alive. Truly alive. Monumental are the contributions that they have made to America, to the world. Remember to keep Italian in your heart and make it always a part of what you do. But always be thoroughly American to the core. It is the journey of the mind, the heart and the soul. It is our faith and history put into action."

It was the immigrants from the village of Caposele who brought their devotion to "Brother Gerard" with them,

Domenico Miano and his bride, Anna Maria Nicola Liloia, were married in the original wood structure of St. Lucy's Church in the Old First Ward in October of 1914. *Courtesy of the Very Reverend Cav. Thomas D. Nicastro, VF.*

as he had not yet been canonized by the Catholic Church. Even though he was not yet a saint, Brother Gerard was celebrated in the Old First Ward.

In October 1904, the Newark newspapers reported that the feast was organized by a group of Caposelesi men led by Gerardo Spatola Sr. This would be the beginning of a long history of members of the Spatola family actively participating in the feast of St. Gerard since its inception in 1899—from Gerardo Spatola Sr. to Gerardo J. Spatola, to daughters Gina and Geta, to Geta's son Gerald.[118] These generations are forever linked to the inception and successful history of the Feast of St. Gerard.

Father Nicastro, along with generations of the immigrants that settled in the Old First Ward when they arrived, follow St. Gerard throughout the streets. While the neighborhood was destroyed in the 1950s due to the development of Route 280 and Newark's urban renewal project, throngs

Gerardo Spatola arrived in Newark in 1880 from Caposele in the province of Avellino. He became a leader in the local Caposelese society and was instrumental in the founding of the Feast of St. Gerard. *Courtesy of Gerard Zanfini and Michael D. Immerso First Ward Italian collection; Charles F. Cummings New Jersey Information Center, Newark Public Library.*

of people still come to St. Lucy's each October and walk in procession. When the procession returns to St. Lucy's and families sit in the pews of the church, they get the opportunity to share the same experience exactly as it happened over one hundred years ago.

"It is the images and the memories that you and I have of our parents and our grandparents and great-grandparents, remembering how they celebrated customs and traditions. It keeps the memory of our ancestors alive," Father Nicastro said. "If any ethnic group is to survive, they must keep alive the parish's spirit and memory from the past as a way to move forward. A deceased loved one's memory is felt keenly inside the church. When that which is holy touches a place, the aura remains long."

Father Nicastro's family, like many of the families from the Old First Ward, goes back to the initial formation of the enclave. It is obvious when speaking with him that his devotion to St. Gerard, coupled with our shared heritage, is a tie that binds everyone from the Old First Ward. His notation

Procession during the Feast of Saint Gerard at the corner of Garside Street and Sixth Avenue, circa 1910. *Courtesy of Gerard Zanfini and Michael D. Immerso First Ward Italian collection; Charles F. Cummings New Jersey Information Center, Newark Public Library.*

of how we, without thinking, refer to our "friend" St. Gerard as "he" is proof of that shared experience.

"Our memory is the most precious faculty. The ability to recall past events. Remember those times we've walked with our relatives in procession, asking for a favor, hoping for some miracle from this great wonder worker," Father Nicastro shared.

I can honestly say when I sit in the quiet of St. Lucy's, I can feel my family sitting around me. During the Feast of St. Gerard, we remember his life and legacy, and we also remember our loved ones and the traditions we were taught as children. And while the Old First Ward is gone, we all still gather once a year and celebrate as a community our devotion to St. Gerard and the longing for a neighborhood destroyed by so-called urban renewal.

This page: The children and grandchildren of the original residents of Old First Ward continue to return each October for the Feast of St. Gerard. The excitement is shared by the crowd as "he" leaves the church and followers begin to process into the streets of the old neighborhood. *Courtesy of Andrea Lyn-Cammarato Van Benschoten.*

OUR LADY OF MOUNT CARMEL

Each summer, Our Lady of Mount Carmel Church in the Ironbound celebrates the feast Chiesa Della Madonna Del Camine. The oldest Italian feast in the Archdiocese of Newark, the annual event was first celebrated in July 1890. Just as the Feast of St. Gerard brings together generations from the Old First Ward in October, the Our Lady of Mount Carmel Feast brings together generations of Italian American families from the Ironbound each July.

Initially, Bishop Wigger wanted to call the parish St. Joseph's, due to the number of parishes already named for Our Lady of Mount Carmel. However, the Italian immigrant community pushed for Our Lady of Mount Carmel. As many southern Italian immigrants left from the port of Naples, it is easy to picture them looking back at the Basilica of Our Lady of Mount Carmel. It could have very well been the last look at their old life before they left the villages their families had lived in for generations. It no doubt left an indelible mark on them. They prayed to Our Lady for a safe journey and for their families. When they arrived in their new communities, these immigrants made good on their prayerful promises and built churches in her honor. The Feast of Our Lady of Mount Carmel is a celebration of their love for the earthly mother of Christ as well as a celebration of their Italian heritage.

The feast was celebrated annually from 1890 until 1967 on Ferry Street. Days before the Our Lady of Mount Carmel feast was to take place in 1967, the Newark Riots erupted. The feast took a very different turn. The

Procession in honor of Our Lady of Mount Carmel, circa 1950. *Courtesy of the* Italian Tribune.

Cavaliere Professore Eric Lavin, director of the Archdiocese of Newark's Italian Apostolate, prays before Our Lady of Mount Carmel during the 2022 feast. *Courtesy of Anthony Scillia.*

celebration became far more subdued for several years. Many Italians who had been part of the Ironbound community for generations chose to leave. As they did in the other Italian immigrant neighborhoods in Newark, the riots took a toll on the community.

Over time, the feast began to return, and the event was officially moved to the "new" church on Oliver Street, where it continues to be celebrated over 130 years after the first event.

OTHER FEASTS

While the Feasts of Our Lady of Mount Carmel and St. Gerard have endured for over a century, there were many others that took place through the history of the Italian enclaves of Newark. Just like the villages of their heritage, each community in Italy had its own patron saint. And just as the generations of villagers had before them, residents would bring the saint out of the church and process through the streets, sharing their love and devotion for their special saint. Throughout the warm weather, feasts were celebrated almost every other week. Each town that was represented in sufficient numbers organized a feast to honor their patron saint. The Teorese showed devotion to Saint Nicolo, the Lionese celebrated

Above: Procession of the Feast of St. Anthony in 1906. *Courtesy of Gerard Zanfini and Michael D. Immerso First Ward Italian collection; Charles F. Cummings New Jersey Information Center, Newark Public Library.*

Opposite: Campione's Band processes along Seventh Avenue with the Sons of Italy in 1915. *Courtesy of Gerard Zanfini and Michael D. Immerso First Ward Italian collection; Charles F. Cummings New Jersey Information Center, Newark Public Library.*

Saint Rocco, the Atripaldese celebrated Saint Sabino, Our Lady of the Assumption (La Madonna Assunta di Pienro) was celebrated as patroness of San Fele and Our Lady of the Snows (Maria delle Neve) was revered by the Calabrittani. The feast of Our Lady of the Snows was shown devotion with a procession through the neighborhood as early as 1888.[119]

The society devoted to each patron saint was responsible for the planning and execution of the feast. Just as a family would prepare a home for a holiday, the society would prepare the church and the neighborhood for the feast. This included decorations, planning entertainment, procession plans, food, down to the smallest detail.

Music played an important role in all feasts. A band would accompany the church pastor, altar boys and the faithful and walk along in the procession as the patron saint was caried throughout the streets of the neighborhood. When the saint returned to the church in the evening, a band or orchestra concert would take place, and the evening culminated with a fireworks display.[120]

By far the most inspiring display of faith took place during the Feast for Saint Michael the Archangel, patron of Maddaloni. During the procession, girls dressed as angels were suspended from ropes attached to the fire escapes and glided above the heads of the crowd as the statue passed by. This part of the celebration took place just as it did in the small villages throughout the Mezzogiorno.

"To such customs, the little town of Polizzi Generosa in Sicily added the lowering into the street of children dressed as angels, supported by ropes from the balconies, as the statue was borne past."[121]

The Flight of the Angels during the Feast of Saint Michael the Archangel on Seventh Avenue, near Sheffield Street in 1939. The angels would be pulled across Seventh Avenue by ropes attached to the fire escapes. The two angels pictured are seven-year-old Julie Alfieri Venero and Barbara Onove West. *Courtesy of Gerard Zanfini and Michael D. Immerso First Ward Italian collection; Charles F. Cummings New Jersey Information Center, Newark Public Library.*

The remaining Italian feasts may look somewhat different than they did at their inception over a century ago; however, the core celebration of the patron saint remains the same. Those who no longer live in the neighborhood of their ancestors make their own pilgrimage to pray, connect with their heritage and remember.

ITALIAN AMERICAN APOSTOLATE OF THE ARCHDIOCESE OF NEWARK

The Italian American Apostolate has enjoyed a resurgence as of late. While the organization was dormant for decades, a group of Italian American Catholics, led by Director and Cavaliere Professore Eric Lavin, has been actively advocating for the Italian Catholic community, including working to ensure masses are still celebrated in Italian. Eric is the first layperson to ever head up the organization and has been a strong advocate in the group's revival. The Apostolate's chaplain is the Very Reverend Cavaliere Thomas D. Nicastro, VF.

"A question a lot of people have is if there really is a need and I think that there is a need. I think it's very relevant. There are still a significant amount of Italian language services offered in Bergen, Essex, Hudson and Union Counties and in rebuilding it, I have tapped into an eager, excited, motivated and driven group of Italian Americans. It has really taken on a life of its own," Eric shared. "It's like the Gospel. It's ancient and it's new. We try to present the Gospel in a way to a new audience in a new setting, and it has really expanded."

The Apostolate participates in multiple religious and secular events to bring the Italian American community together, including feasts, processions and bus trips. There is an honest camaraderie among the group members, and they share their faith in a fun way.

"The faith really isn't that hard. What does it mean to be a Christian person? What does Christ teach us? Care for the neighbor, welcome the stranger, care for the sick, these are things that should be inherent in every person," Eric explained. "And we add the interest of our culture, and a twist of heritage, and that's the Italian Apostolate."

Italian American Apostolate in the Italian immigrant Chapel at the Cathedral Basilica of the Sacred Heart at the Chrism Mass, March 25, 2024. *Courtesy of Italian Apostolate member Danielle Gherardi.*

The ministry has made huge strides in a short amount of time. They have assembled a list of Italian-speaking priests in the archdiocese, they help the elderly contact priests if last rites are needed and they welcomed a group of musicians from Monte San Giacomo in Campania for the first time to perform in the Cathedral Basilica of the Sacred Heart for Christmas.

The cathedral is also a source of pride for the Italian immigrant community of New Jersey.

"That cathedral was built by Italian immigrants," Eric said. "In the cathedral is represented and memorialized all the ethnic groups that built it in individual chapels. We have St. Lucy Filippini, Mother Cabrini and St. Gerard in our chapel. These saints, they tell part of the story, especially in this corner of New Jersey."

As we concluded our conversation, Eric told me a funny story about the initial meetings of Italian Apostolate.

"When we first started our Apostolate meetings, we didn't have any food. By our third meeting, we decided we needed food at every meeting," Eric joked. "Food is always a big motivator for us."

Faith, family and food. That is our mantra.

10
IN CLOSING

W here do we go from here?

For those of us of Italian heritage, we have a responsibility. Our story deserves to be told. And to paraphrase a line that is often repeated on *The Italian American Podcast*, if we don't tell our story, no one else will. We need to collectively, as a community, take a stand, join local organizations and help plan and lead events.

So, ask questions of your family elders. Write names, dates and locations on the back of each photo you find. Like many others, I take painstaking measures to document my family history, our heritage and the profound effect it has had on me. I work equally as hard to understand that heritage and how it has been adapted over the years. When did something "Italian" become "Italian American"? What is our story? I do this to not just remember and honor those who came before me but with the hope someone down the line will want to know these stories and have interest in all the information that has been collected.

The most important step we can all take as Americans of Italian descent is learn about our history. Share it with family and friends. We are here because of the risks and hard work of those who came before us. We need to, as my Uncle Chubby often reminded us, "never forget where you came from."

Throughout this project, I discovered several common themes. What might be the most important one, however, is that there seems to be one member of a family who takes the time to document family stories and

Gabriel Anthony "Chubby" Fieramosco (stage name: Chubby O'Dell), a member of Chubby O'Dell and the Blue Mountain Boys, posing with his son, Patrick Anthony "Patty Boy" Fieramosco. Uncle Chubby, as he was known to family, friends and loved ones, reminded all of us growing up to never forget where we came from. *Courtesy Andrea Lyn Cammarato-Van Benschoten.*

histories. The one who researches their family's original villages. I urge you to be that person.

I will also tell you, there are individuals who think your effort is a waste of time. That will scoff at your work. Here is my advice: find your own people and forge your own group of paesani. Find those who share your passion. Look for those who will encourage instead of making wisecracks and disparaging comments.

We have a story to tell. We need to tell it.

So, whenever you get discouraged, remember that you are not just writing for now. You are writing for the future in the hope someone will want to read what you have collected and written.

May you find your paesani and be encouraged.

Modern-Day Resources

If I have piqued your interest, wonderful! I hope you will learn more and look for more information about Italian history, heritage, culture, the immigration story to America and our unique story in this country.

There is a wide variety of resources available today in an array of formats covering a dizzying collection of subjects. This is far from an exhaustive list, but it includes sources I have listened to and read in preparation for this project as well as podcasts, newspapers and books I refer to regularly.

Podcasts

Breaking Bread
The Italian American Podcast
Italian Roots and Genealogy

Books

Aprile, Pino. *Terroni: All That Has Been Done to Ensure That the Italians of the South Became "Southerners."* New York: Bordighera Press, 2011.

Cole, Trafford Robertson. *Italian Genealogical Records: How to Use Italian Civil, Ecclesiastical and Other Records in Family History Research.* Salt Lake City, UT: Ancestry, 1995.

DiStasi, Lawrence, ed. *Una Storia Segreta: The Secret History of Italian American Evacuation and Internment during World War II.* Berkeley, CA: Heyday, 2001.

Eula, Michael J. *Between Peasant and Urban Villager: Italian-Americans of New Jersey and New York, 1880–1980: The Structures of Counter-Discourse*. New York: P. Lang, 1993.

Fox, Stephen. *The Unknown Internment: An Oral History of the Relocation of Italian Americans during World War II*. Boston: Twayne Publishers, 1990.

Immerso, Michael. *Newark's Little Italy: The Vanished First Ward*. New Brunswick, NJ: Rutgers University Press, 1997.

Lee, Sandra S., PhD. *Italian Americans of Newark, Belleville, and Nutley*. Charleston, SC: Arcadia Publishing, 2008.

Mangione, Jerre, and Ben Morreale. *La Storia: Five Centuries of the Italian American Experience*. New York: Harper Collins Publishing, 1992.

Nelli, Humbert S. *From Immigrants to Ethnics*. Oxford, UK: Oxford University Press, 1983.

Nicastro, Reverend Thomas D., V.F. *The Feast of St. Gerard Maiella, C.Ss.R.: A Century of Devotion at St. Lucy's, Newark*. Charleston, SC: The History Press, 2012.

Ranu, Jennifer Tiritilli. *Italians of Greater Paterson*. Charleston, SC: Arcadia Publishing, 2019.

Starr, Dennis J. *The Italians of New Jersey: A Historical Introduction and Bibliography*. Newark, NJ: New Jersey Historical Society, 1985.

Sullivan, Mary Louise, MSC. *Mother Cabrini: Italian Immigrant of the Century*. New York: Center for Migration Studies, 1992.

Newspapers/Websites

America Oggi
Italian Tribune
Jersey Girl, Italian Roots
We the Italians

Organizations

Apostolato Italiano dell'Arcidiocesi di Newark/Italian Apostolate RCAN
Coccia Foundation
Filitalia International
Italian American Museum
Italian American One Voice Coalition
Italian Genealogy Society of NJ
Italian Sons and Daughters of America (ISDA)
National Italian American Foundation (NIAF)
New Jersey Italian Heritage Commission
Newark First Ward Heritage and Cultural Society/First Ward Museum
Order Sons and Daughters of Italy in America (OSDIA)
Spilingese Social Club–Newark
UNICO National (Unity, Neighborliness, Integrity, Charity and Opportunity)

NOTES

Introduction

1. Dennis J. Starr, *The Italians of New Jersey: A Historical Introduction and Bibliography* (Newark, NJ: New Jersey Historical Society, 1985), i.
2. Library of Congress, "Immigration to the United States, 1851–1900," www.loc.gov.
3. Walter F. Willcox, *International Migrations*, vol. 2, *Interpretations* (Cambridge, MA: National Bureau of Economic Research, 1931), 177–78.
4. Douglas V. Shaw, *Immigration and Ethnicity in New Jersey History* (Trenton, NJ: New Jersey Historical Commission, 1994), 10.
5. Luciano Iorizzo and Salvatore Mondello, *The Italian Americans* (Youngstown, NY: Cambria Press, 2006), 286–87.

Chapter 1

6. Joseph Lopreato, *Peasants No More: Social Class and Social Change in an Underdeveloped Society* (San Francisco: Chandler Publishing, 1963), 6.
7. Robert Corbo, "Italian Settlements in Newark, New Jersey" (diss., East Carolina University, Department of Geography, 1975), 45.
8. Lucy Riall, *Risorgimento* (New York: Palgrave Macmillan, 2009), 37–38.
9. Jerre Mangione and Ben Morreale, *La Storia: Five Centuries of the Italian American Experience* (New York: Harper Collins Publishing, 1992), 39.
10. Ibid., 55.

11. Riall, *Risorgimento*, 45.
12. Mangione and Morreale, *La Storia*, 62.
13. Ibid., 67.
14. Humbert S. Nelli, *From Immigrants to Ethnics* (Oxford, UK: Oxford University Press, 1983), 20.
15. Mangione and Morreale, *La Storia*, 75.
16. Ibid.
17. Mangione and Morreale, *La Storia*, 73.
18. Ibid., 63.
19. Ibid., 69.
20. Nelli, *From Immigrants to Ethnics*, 23.
21. Mangione and Morreale, *La Storia*, 69.
22. Library of Congress, "Immigration and Relocation in U.S. History," www.loc.gov.
23. Ibid.
24. Starr, *Italians of New Jersey*, 3.
25. Library of Congress, "Ellis Island," www.loc.gov.
26. Statue of Liberty Ellis Island Foundation, "Sailing to the Land of Liberty," www.statueofliberty.org.
27. Alexander De Conde, *Half Bitter, Half Sweet: An Excursion into Italian American History* (New York: Scribner, 1971), 72.
28. Mangione and Morreale, *La Storia*, 112.
29. Corbo, "Italian Settlements in Newark," 66.
30. Starr, *Italians of New Jersey*, 7.
31. Corbo, "Italian Settlements in Newark," 44.
32. Internet Archive, "A Map of Newark with Areas Where Different Nationalities Predominate," https://archive.org.
33. Corbo, "Italian Settlements in Newark," 66.
34. Ibid., 32.

Chapter 2

35. Italian Sons and Daughters of America, "Mobster Joke Lands Prominent NJ Reporter in Hot Seat," https://orderisda.org.
36. Giuseppe Piccoli, "Italian Immigration in the United States" (master's thesis, Duquesne University, 2014).
37. Immigration Restriction League Records, 1893–1921 (MS Am 2245), Houghton Library, Harvard University.
38. W.P. Dillingham, "Immigrants in Industries (in Twenty-Five Parts)," Reports of the Immigration Commission, Senate Document no. 633, 61st

Congress, 2nd Session (Washington, D.C.: Government Printing Office, 1911), 25.

39. Ibid.

40. Ibid.

41. History, "Immigration Act Passed Over President Wilson's Veto," www.history.com.

42. Walter A. Montgomery, *Education in Italy*, no. 36 (Washington, D.C.: Department of the Interior Bureau of Education, 1919).

43. Department of Labor, *Immigration and Passenger Movement: Total Number of Immigrants in Specified Years*, Reports of the Commissioner General of Immigration, No. 63.

44. Albert Johnson and David Reed, *The Immigration Act of 1924*, 1924, enacted by the 68th United States Congress, introduced in the House of Representatives as H.R. 7995.

45. Graziano Battistella, "Italian Immigrants to the United States: The Last Twenty Years," Center for Migration Studies special issues (1989): 1.

46. Una Storia Segreta, "Don't Speak the Enemy's Language," www.unastoriasegreta.com/restrictions/language.

47. National Archives, "Executive Order 9066: Resulting in Japanese-American Internment," www.archives.gov.

48. Ibid.

49. Italian Sons and Daughters of America, "Joe DiMaggio Was an Icon, His Father Was an Outcast," www.orderisda.org.

50. James Rowe Jr., "The Alien Enemy Program—So Far," *Common Ground Summer* (1942): 19.

51. Stephen C. Fox, *The Unknown Internment: An Oral History of the Relocation of Italian Americans during World War II* (Boston: Twayne, 1990), 144.

52. Smithsonian, "During World War II, the U.S. Saw Italian-Americans as a Threat to Homeland Security." www.smithsonianmag.com.

53. Italian Sons and Daughters of America, "Italian American Heroes Who Made World War II History," www.orderisda.org.

54. Ibid.

55. "V.F.W. to Name Post for Jos. R. Rotunda," *Italian Tribune*, February 25, 1944.

Chapter 3

56. Michael Immerso, *Newark's Little Italy: The Vanished First Ward* (New Brunswick, NJ: Rutgers University Press, 1997), 5.

57. Ibid., 5.

58. Ibid., 16.

59. Ibid., 140.

60. Brad R. Tuttle, *How Newark Became Newark: The Rise, Fall, and Rebirth of an American City* (New Brunswick, NJ: Rutgers University Press, 2009), 139.

61. Immerso, *Newark's Little Italy*, 140.

62. Tuttle, *How Newark Became Newark*, 134.

Chapter 4

63. Edward A. Jardim, *The Ironbound: An Illustrated History of Newark's "Down Neck"* (Frenchtown, NJ: Stone Creek Publications, 2016), 31.

64. Ibid.

65. Ibid., 21.

66. Charles Wesley Churchill, *The Italians in Newark: A Community Study* (New York: Arno Press, 1975), 91 (Churchill's dissertation was originally completed in 1940).

67. Michael J. Eula, *Between Peasant and Urban Villager: Italian-Americans of New Jersey and New York, 1880–1980: The Structures of Counter* (New York: Peter Land, 1993), 29.

Chapter 5

68. Michael Immerso, *Enclaves of Memory*, program of the Newark History Society (Newark Public Library, 2019).

69. "Pennsylvania Has Bought More Land," *Newark Evening News*, June 27, 1902.

70. Old Newark, "Silver Lake," https://oldnewark.com.

Chapter 6

71. La Voce di New York, "Italian Media in the United States: A Two-Century-Long History," https://lavocedinewyork.com.

72. Rudolph J. Vecoli, *The People of New Jersey* (New Princeton, NJ: Van Nostrand, 1965), 226.

73. Churchill, *Italians in Newark*, 163.

74. Vince Tuzzolo, "All in a Week," *Italian Tribune*, March 8, 1968.

Chapter 7

75. Vecoli, *People of New Jersey*, 229.
76. Ibid.
77. Starr, *Italians of New Jersey*, 23.
78. Churchill, *Italians in Newark*, 40.
79. Ibid., 132.

Chapter 8

80. Ian MacAllen, *Red Sauce* (Lanham, MD: Rowman & Littlefield, 2022).
81. Mangione and Morreale, *La Storia*, 35.
82. Ibid., 39.

Chapter 9

83. New Jersey Catholic Historical Records Commission, *The Bishops of Newark, 1853–1978* (South Orange, NJ: Seton Hall University Press, 1978), 44.
84. Eula, *Between Peasant and Urban Villager*, 238.
85. Churchill, *Italians in Newark*, 91.
86. Eula, *Between Peasant and Urban Villager*, 239.
87. New Jersey Catholic Historical Records Commission, *Bishops of Newark*, 59.
88. Ibid.
89. Ibid.
90. Churchill, *Italians in Newark*, 95.
91. Ibid., 97.
92. 132nd Annual Feast of Our Lady of Mount Carmel annual program.
93. Churchill, *Italians in Newark*, 97.
94. 132nd Annual Feast of Our Lady of Mount Carmel annual program.
95. Ibid.
96. Ibid.
97. Mary Louise Sullivan, *Mother Cabrini, "Italian Immigrant of the Century"* (United States: Center for Migration Studies, 1992), 156.
98. Ibid., 177.
99. 132nd Annual Feast of Our Lady of Mount Carmel annual program.
100. Ibid.
101. Immerso, *Newark's Little Italy*, 65.

102. Reverend Thomas D. Nicastro, *The Feast of St. Gerard Maiella, C.Ss.R.: A Century of Devotion at St. Lucy's, Newark, New Jersey* (Charleston, SC: The History Press, 2012), 33.
103. Immerso, *Newark's Little Italy*, 66.
104. Ibid.
105. Immerso, *Newark's Little Italy*, 67.
106. Nicastro, *Feast of St. Gerard Maiella*, 81.
107. Ibid., 76.
108. Monsignor Joseph Granato, interview in documentary, *The One Hundred Year Anniversary of the Feast of St. Gerard.*
109. Nicastro, *Feast of St. Gerard Maiella*, 34.
110. Churchill, *Italians in Newark*, 26–27.
111. Ibid., 102.
112. Ibid.
113. National Register of Historic Places Inventory Nomination Form, St. Rocco's Roman Catholic Church, Essex County, 1980.
114. Corbo, "Italian Settlements in Newark," 47.
115. Eula, *Between Peasant and Urban Villager*, 239.
116. Immerso, *Newark's Little Italy*, 81.
117. Nicastro, *Feast of St. Gerard Maiella*, 34.
118. Ibid., 38.
119. Immerso, *Newark's Little Italy*, 82.
120. Ibid., 83.
121. Phyllis H. Williams, *South Italian Folkways in Europe and America: A Handbook for Social Workers, Visiting Nurses, School Teachers, and Physicians* (New Haven, CT: Yale University Press, 1938), 140.

INDEX

ABOUT THE AUTHOR

Andrea Lyn Cammarato-Van Benschoten was born in Columbus Hospital in Newark and grew up one town over in Belleville. A Jersey girl with a passion for her Italian heritage, she was taught at a young age to "never forget where you came from." For her, that goes back to Campania and Sicily, to the Old First Ward of Newark. Andrea studied journalism at Seton Hall University and writes multiple blogs, including one about her beloved New Jersey and one about her Italian heritage. She lives with her husband of thirty years, Glenn, in Morris County, New Jersey.